"Rebecca Ingram Powell has written the best new mom's journal on the market today. Reading *Baby Boot Camp*, a new mom will find a friend and mentor who jumps down in the trenches with her. I truly believe that *Baby Boot Camp* should be tucked in every new mom's diaper bag!"

—Lysa TerKeurst,
president of Proverbs 31 Ministries
and author of *Capture His Heart*

"Wonderfully encouraging devotionals . . . for the first six weeks and beyond!"

—Karyn Henley,
author of *The Beginner's Bible*

"The First Orlando Foundation has been blessed by the feedback we have received from young mothers and moms-to-be regarding *Baby Boot Camp*. We have distributed this wonderful tool primarily through our First Life Center for Pregnancy and recommend it highly!"

—Randall James, President,
First Orlando Foundation

"No one is really able to adequately prepare for the joys and trials of motherhood, yet now there is a guide to help you navigate the land mines and embrace the triumphs. In *Baby Boot Camp*, Rebecca Ingram Powell gives real-life advice for real-life mothers. Most importantly, she recognizes that new moms are first and foremost spiritual beings that need nourishment, and she provides just that. I try to make sure all my new moms leave the hospital with a copy of *Baby Boot Camp*."

—J. Ron Eaker, M.D.,
obstetrician-gynecologist
and author of *Holy Hormones!*

BABY
BOOT
CAMP

BABY
BOOT
CAMP

Basic Training for the First
Six Weeks of Motherhood

By Rebecca Ingram Powell

new
hope
PUBLISHERS

Birmingham, Alabama

New Hope® Publishers
P. O. Box 12065
Birmingham, AL 35202-2065
www.newhopepubl.com

Library of Congress Cataloging-in-Publication Data
Powell, Rebecca Ingram.
Baby boot camp : basic training for the first six weeks of
motherhood / by Rebecca Ingram Powell.
p. cm.
ISBN 1-56309-820-2 (softcover)
1. Mothers-Religious life. 2. Motherhood-Religious aspects-Chris-
tianity. 3. Mother and infant. I. Title.
BV4529.18.P678 2004
242'.6431—dc22
2003021028

ISBN: 1-56309-820-2

N044108 • 0104 • 7.5M1

Dedication

*Lovingly dedicated to
my mother: Mary Lou Ingram
and my mother-in-law: Patricia Powell*

Table of Contents

Foreword

Hosting and producing national television shows did little to prepare me for motherhood! Experiencing childbirth, a C-section, and the weeks and months that followed left me feeling like I had entered a war zone with extreme battle fatigue—physically, mentally, and spiritually. *Baby Boot Camp* would have provided me with the ammunition I needed in order to have walked in victory sooner.

Baby Boot Camp shines the spotlight on the realities all women face as new moms. Now as they prepare to enter the toughest and most rewarding war they will ever wage, they don't have to feel isolated and alone. *Baby Boot Camp* is an uplifting devotional filled with faith-building stories and Scriptures as well as a practical survival guide that will help new moms make the most of motherhood. With pages packed with wisdom, knowledge, and practical tips, *Baby Boot Camp* is a must-read for new moms!

Debra Maffett Wilson
Miss America 1983

Acknowledgments

Thank You, God, for

• My wonderful husband, who faithfully supports me in all my endeavors. You are my best friend, Rich, and I love you.

• My children, who play together quietly when Mom is writing on the computer. Danya, David, and Derek, you are gifts from God, and I am so blessed to be your mother. I love you! Without you, this book could have never been written!

• Ginger Moore and Sondra Dean, whose pregnancies provided the dream, the desire, and the deadline for writing *Baby Boot Camp.*

• Lorie Barber and Micca Campbell, who pray with me and for me, and the many other prayer partners who have earnestly prayed over *Baby Boot Camp.*

• Dr. Rick Barkley, whose lay-sermon about Omaha Beach came along at precisely the right time.

• Jon and Sherry Walker, who share their talents so graciously and their friendship so lovingly with Rich and me.

• Jeff and Rhonda Morris, for their friendship, prayers, and support.

• My parents, Rev. and Mrs. Ted J. Ingram, whose Christianity lived before me daily was the most profound influence on my life.

• And most of all, for the Lord Jesus Christ, who calls the *unlikely* to do the *unimaginable* with *unbeatable* results!

Introduction

Dear Friend,

Congratulations! If you're reading this book, you're a new mom. Your baby is beautiful. Children are a blessing from God. He loves you, and He loves your baby, too.

This book is written for you. My goal in writing it has been to help you through the first six weeks of your baby's life. There are 42 devotions, with Scripture included, to get you through this wonderful time that I affectionately refer to as "boot camp."

It's important that you take a few moments each day for yourself. Read the day's Scripture and devotional, and enjoy a quiet time with God to think and reflect and pray. Before you know it, these first six weeks will be a memory.

Baby Boot Camp was written with you in mind. I remember so many moments during the first six weeks with each of my three children when I simply longed for some encouragement. My prayer is that God will speak to you through the pages of this book, and most importantly, through the portion of His Word that precedes each devotion. May it be exactly what you need, encouraging you through the days ahead.

God bless you and your baby,
Rebecca

P.S. The devotions for Day 5, Day 7, and Day 8

include my children's "life verses." These are verses that my husband and I asked the Lord for prior to each child's birth. We had these certain Scriptures printed on their birth announcements, and they have become lifelong prayers for each child. I encourage you to seek a "life verse" for your baby. Make it a nightly blessing, a daily song, and a lifetime promise for your little one.

Welcome to Fort Baby

"Sons are a heritage from the LORD,
children a reward from him.
Like arrows in the hands of a warrior
are sons born in one's youth.
Blessed is the man
whose quiver is full of them.
They will not be put to shame
when they contend with their enemies in the gate."
—*Psalm 127:3–5*

When our oldest child was born, our insurance allowed for only one night's stay at the hospital. Danielle Grace Powell, "Danya," was born at 10:17 P.M., and we were back home by one o'clock the following afternoon. Totally drained, I barely remember anything about that homecoming except that our Sunday School class had decorated the door of our apartment with pink streamers and balloons. It was a heartwarming touch, and it welcomed the three of us home. We immediately went to lie down, all of us exhausted.

I recall waking up to a severe pounding on the front door. It sounded as though someone was trying to knock it down! Rich jumped up and raced to the door. As I slowly began making my way down the hall, I heard him talking to our neighbors, a young couple with a little girl about 18 months old. They were explaining that they had come upstairs earlier and knocked on our door, but no one answered. Then they tried phoning us, but again no answer. They had seen our car and all the decorations and had become worried, knowing we were just home from the hospital. So they had come back upstairs and begun literally beating on the door. We were so tired that we hadn't heard the phone or their knocking.

They brought with them a bowl of piping hot spaghetti, freshly baked bread, and homemade brownies. What a wonderful, thoughtful gift of neighborly hospitality. And oddly enough, we really didn't know this couple very well. Yet this young woman put herself in my place, saw my need, and met it. She remembered what having a new baby was like. She had been there. *She knew.*

Now I've been where you are, new mom. In fact, I've been there three times. I have often referred to these first six weeks with a new baby as "boot camp." So welcome to Fort Baby!

It's tough.

It is a time of strict training and discipline.

It is preparation for the life ahead.

It is a grounding of your heart, mind, and soul.

It is learning to think of another before you

think of yourself.

But the best part about this boot camp is that you don't have to struggle through it alone. Jesus Christ wants to walk the floor with you, climb the walls with you, jump for joy with you, and run the race with you. Maybe you haven't really noticed Him, as I hadn't noticed my neighbor. I knew she was there, but spending time with her wasn't really on my schedule. I was so busy coming and going that I never stopped to talk to her beyond an occasional greeting. But she had good things for me! She knew what I needed, exactly when I needed it. I was sorry it took so long for her to get my attention.

Perhaps this book will serve as a wake-up call to you. God may not pound on the door of your heart, but He certainly has His ways of waking us up. Like my neighbor, He has only good things for you, new mom, wonderful things—like the touchable, lovable, adorable blessing of a child. Who can fathom this great reward? This is your heritage from the Lord, straight from His riches in glory!

Please rest and enjoy this first night home together as a family. Savor the feeling of this first night because soon you won't be able to remember what it was like to have an empty house.

Revel in the contrast of empty versus full.

Marvel at the difference between two and three!

Mark it in your memory to cherish forever.

First Night Home

Quiet, quiet, Baby's sleeping!
Softly 'round her, angels creeping—
Gently now, they tiptoe, sigh,
And crowd her room with lullaby.

Their voices warm like summer wind.
Like shepherds to sheep, my baby they tend.
Whispering medley, so thickly sweet,
Like Baby's breath: delicate, deep.

Creaking rocker accompanies
The band of angels' harmonies.
My heart has never heard such sounds:
The rhapsody of seven pounds!

The homecoming is oh, so sweet,
And now our lives are so complete.
We join Zion's chorus, praising Christ!
He's blessed our love with this new life.

His promised guardians surround her bed
As I lay down her precious head.
Celestial nursery, joy once unknown—
Heaven on earth: her first night home!

❤

**Praise God in advance for all He will be
teaching you in the days ahead.**

Enlisted

"Then God said, 'Let us make man in our image, in our like-ness, and let them rule over the fish of the sea and the birds of the air, over the livestock, over all the earth, and over all the creatures that move along the ground.' So God created man in his own image, in the image of God he created him; **male and female he created them. . . . the LORD God formed the man from the dust of the ground and breathed into his nostrils the breath of life, and the man became a living being."**

—Genesis 1:26–27, 2:7

How difficult it is to wait for a new baby! It is a sweet time of wondering, wishing, and want-ing. You wonder what this little person will be like, from gender to personality to fingers and toes. You wish for that due date to come quickly, and as it does, you want to be prepared.

Getting the baby's nursery ready takes up a lot of time, and it's a great outlet for eager parents. Once Rich and I got the crib assembled and in its place, we made it a part of our nightly routine to walk in that little room, still and sterile in its newness, and look at everything before we went to bed. Family and friends had so generously showered us with gifts that I was hard-pressed to find something we had bought ourselves. How many times I must have smoothed out the little comforter on that baby's bed, tenderly spun the mobile, adjusted the cushion on the rocking chair, and made sure I had the diapers and wipes just so on the changing table. I thought that our nursery was fully dressed, finished, and just waiting for a baby. What I didn't realize was how naked, incomplete, and empty it was—until that baby came home from the hospital, and through her, God breathed the breath of life into our little nursery. What a mind-boggling revelation!

Once you know that baby is coming, there is a void that grows more empty as that belly grows fuller and a longing that becomes more intense with the passing of each day. It's an ever-increasing longing, resonating from the very heart of your feminine being, to hold and kiss and stroke and communicate with this stranger you know so well. Until that baby is born, it just feels like something's missing.

In a similar way, there comes a point in each person's life when she realizes that truly, something *is* missing. It is our human nature to try filling that emptiness with different things: other people, possessions, prominence, pleasure. But nothing will fill that empty place because, you see, that longing is coming from your spirit, and your spirit won't be satisfied with anything but Jesus. That emptiness is simply a recognition of a separation that exists between you and God, your Creator. It occurred as a result of sin, our disobedience in holding to the standards of a righteous God. Sin separates us from a relationship with God, but it doesn't separate us from His love! He proved that He loved us, and He calls us to come to Him by way of His Son, Jesus Christ. Jesus died on the cross to cleanse us from our sins, to re-establish our relationship with God, and to cover us with His righteousness.

A celebrity interviewer was himself interviewed on a popular talk show a few years ago. He was asked who, in his opinion, would be the ultimate interview. He replied that he would like to interview God.

"What would you ask him?" the host said.

Without a moment's hesitation, the man replied, "Did you have a son?"

Even this man who asks all the questions has one for which his heart cries out for an answer, and in his life there will always be a certain emptiness without Jesus Christ.

Just as your nursery knows new life now that its occupant has arrived, you also can experience new life in Christ if you allow Him to reside in your heart. God did have a Son! His name is Jesus. The Bible says, *"For God so loved the world that he gave his one and only Son, that whoever believes in him shall not perish but have eternal life"* (John 3:16).

If you do not know Jesus Christ as your personal Savior, please allow Him access to your heart of hearts this moment. Recognize that your sin has left you in dire need of a Savior, and accept His free gift of salvation. If you've never asked Jesus to forgive you of your sins, all it takes is a prayer. He's waiting for you with open arms.

Dear God, I realize that I need You. Please forgive me of my sins. I believe that Jesus is Your Son, and I ask Him now to come into my heart and fill up this emptiness with His love. I want Jesus to be my Savior and Lord. In Jesus' name, Amen.

Even as your baby fits inside your arms just perfectly, so you, as a child of God, will fit into His. Let Him help you be the woman He wants you to be.

❤

Victory lies in a heart surrendered to the Savior.

Military Time

"There is a time for everything,
and a season for every activity under heaven:
a time to be born and a time to die,
a time to plant and a time to uproot,
a time to kill and a time to heal,
a time to tear down and a time to build,
a time to weep and a time to laugh,
a time to mourn and a time to dance,
a time to scatter stones and a time to gather them,
a time to embrace and a time to refrain,
a time to search and a time to give up,
a time to keep and a time to throw away,
a time to tear and a time to mend,
a time to be silent and a time to speak,
a time to love and a time to hate,
a time for war and a time for peace.

*What does the worker gain from his toil? I have seen the burden God has laid on men. **He has made everything beautiful in its time.** He has also set eternity in the hearts of men; yet they cannot fathom what God has done from beginning to end."*

—Ecclesiastes 3:1–11

The honesty of the writer of Ecclesiastes is refreshing. God was good to include that person's soul-searching struggle in His Word. Here's someone who has lived his life and now, as he reaches the end of it, seeks to share his experience—what worked and what didn't, what was real treasure and what would fade away, what was futile and what was forever. He uses simple yet beautiful language to advise people of the hope of God amid the shortness of life and remind us of the essence of time. It's odd how we underestimate the true value of time until we have only a very little of it left.

Like a young soldier, a mother finds herself adjusting to a new standard of time. Babies are indifferent to A.M. and P.M. Like our armed forces, they prefer a twenty-four-hour clock. Lots of jokes are made about our country's use of military time, but while it seems strange and perplexing to us, our soldiers have learned it, and they use it primarily to *avoid* confusion. God's timing is the same way: it is foreign to us, but if we could only learn it and use it, we would avoid much of the confusion in our lives.

Anne Ortlund writes in her book *Children Are Wet Cement*, "God is wonderful about developing our gifts according to His own schedule for our lives. He knows which are the years when there is no substitute for parenting. It's the job that must be done then, not later. It's when the cement is wet."

There *is* a time for everything. God has planned for that. He has ordained each hour of life, especially this time of parenting. We serve a God who wants to reveal His true nature to us; therefore, He constantly refers to Himself as Father. We need to understand that role, and now is the time that God Himself will show you—sometimes in startlingly brilliant revelations—His Father-love. Once these days are gone, they will not be regained. Like wet cement, all that will remain are the imprints we have made. Those imprints will show our children and future generations what we considered important.

How quickly this time with your newborn will pass! And then will come those wonderful growing-up years. What a precious gift that God has given you—this time, this beautiful season of life. Spring has bloomed in your home, and the new life you hold in your arms is indeed your heritage from the Lord. This time you have as a mother, though it can never be repossessed, is an investment that will be returned in eternity. How will you spend it?

❤

**Pray today for the imprint of Christ
on your child's parents.**

Calisthenics

"Do you not know that in a race all the runners run, but only one gets the prize? Run in such a way as to get the prize. **Everyone who competes in the games goes into strict training. They do it to get a crown that will not last; but we do it to get a crown that will last forever.** *Therefore I do not run like a man running aimlessly; I do not fight like a man beating the air. No, I beat my body and make it my slave so that after I have preached to others, I myself will not be disqualified for the prize."*
—I Corinthians 9:24–27

The apostle Paul often uses athletic parallels in describing the Christian life. Olympic athletes, of course, must train their bodies extensively, undergoing grueling workouts, if they hope to win the gold medal. If you've ever seen Olympians interviewed on television, most of them admit that their sport has been their life's focus for as long as they can remember. They have surrendered their lives and their youth for a chance at earthly victory, and they have sacrificed dearly with their own flesh in training.

In God's great scheme of things, we women have nine months to prepare for a baby. That's the time allotted, on average, to prepare heart, mind, and home for the precious life forming inside the womb. The Lord Himself prepares your body. Have you survived nausea, leg cramps, mood swings, and other previously unimagined horrors? It all had to happen as a primer for the ultimate endurance test of labor and delivery. New mothers readily admit it was all worth it.

Now that the baby is home, and bewilderment has set in, you may be thinking, *But what do I know about this? I'm a first-time mom! Sure, my body survived labor and delivery, but now what? I hardly know how to change diapers! I'm not prepared to raise a child!* Rest assured, God has choreographed every moment of your life, every experience, every circumstance, and He has led you to this moment in time. He has always known you would be the mother of this child.

The Lord continues to teach you. The first six weeks are especially tough as He gives you a crash course in servanthood, your own personal boot camp for moms. Your body continues to be tried as healing begins (is there an ice pack between your legs?) and hormones readjust. If you're nursing, get ready for sore nipples and leaky breasts, along with intense uterine cramps. More mood swings are on the way, with postpartum depression at the front lines. Your drill sergeant wears a diaper and screams every command, waking you at all hours of the night and keeping you on your toes all day.

You will literally lay down your life during this time, Mom. Let it bring you closer to the One who laid down His life for you.

♥

Pray today for a closer walk with Jesus.

Basic Training

"This is the message we have heard from him and declare to you: God is light; in him there is no darkness at all. If we claim to have fellowship with him yet walk in the darkness, we lie and do not live by the truth. ***But if we walk in the light, as he is in the light, we have fellowship with one another, and the blood of Jesus, his Son, purifies us from all sin.***

"If we claim to be without sin, we deceive ourselves and the truth is not in us. If we confess our sins, he is faithful and just and will forgive us our sins and purify us from all unrighteousness."

—I John 1:5–9

A few days after we arrived home from the hospital, it became apparent that Danya had her days and nights mixed up. I really shouldn't have been surprised. She was born at 10:17 P.M., so that's when her first "day" started. She was awake—bathing, nursing, meeting new people—that first night (when we both should have been sleeping), so when morning came along, she then started her "night."

I was totally baffled. What do I do? Even as a new mom, I was already convinced that the old adage, "Never wake a sleeping baby" had its merits! But every mom I asked for advice told me that in my case, I had better wake that baby. So I did, and I began to do several things that I hoped would help her distinguish the day from the night.

First, I opened all the curtains and mini-blinds as soon as I woke up in the mornings, even going in Danya's room to open hers and let the sunshine wake her. I turned on the radio or played music and began working about the house so she would soon equate activity with daytime behavior. At naptime and bedtime, however, the house was much more quiet and peaceful. Curtains were drawn, the lights were low, and the only noises were the quiet hum of the dishwasher or the murmur of whatever ballgame Rich was watching. I did everything I could to draw a sharp contrast between day and night for my child. I realized then, just scratching the surface of life with a newborn, that I was already her teacher! That heady discovery was quickly met with a heartfelt burden of the responsibility it carried.

Today, of course, Danya knows the difference between day and night, and as a baby, she settled into a regular daytime schedule pretty easily. My job, all too quickly, evolved from teaching her those basics of living to teaching her the basics of life. You see, Christian parenting is about drawing a distinction for your child between the light of Christ Jesus and the darkness of evil in the world. Unfortunately, it is not a lesson accomplished with words as much as one achieved with action; truly, it *is* caught, not taught. I whispered to that sleeping baby girl vivid descriptions of the beautiful day she was missing. But I had to *show* her the sunshine before she would stay awake to enjoy it.

In the same way, my life—my walk with Christ that I model before my children—must be one that is clear-cut. I don't want to send any mixed signals. I can't look like the world and act like the world and still expect to show my kids who Jesus is. But if I'm walking in His light and resting in His love, they'll see the difference.

Your baby *will* sleep through the night soon, and she *will* develop a schedule, and you *will* adapt as you adopt your own personal style of mothering. Be encouraged; God will help you. You will do a great job!

❤

Walk in His light today, and rest in His love.

Danya's life verse: *"Thou art worthy, O Lord, to receive glory and honor and power: for thou hast created all things, and for thy pleasure they are and were created."*

—*Revelation 4:11 KJV*

The Hero

*"Do not store up for yourselves treasures on earth, where moth and rust destroy, and where thieves break in and steal. But **store up for yourselves treasures in heaven,** where moth and rust do not destroy, and where thieves do not break in and steal. For where your treasure is, there your heart will be also."*

—Matthew 6:19–21

Lieutenant Audie Murphy was the favorite son of Farmersville, Texas. An orphaned son of poor sharecroppers, he gained notoriety while serving as a combat soldier during World War II. On January 26, 1945, Lt. Murphy saved his entire company from an attack by six tanks and two hundred fifty German infantrymen. At the risk of his own life, he jumped onto a burning tank destroyer and used its machine gun to kill the enemy troops. For this he received the Congressional Medal of Honor, this nation's highest military award. By the tender age of 21, the courageous Lt. Murphy had received every decoration for valor that this country had to offer, including five additional honors from France and Belgium. He became America's most decorated soldier of World War II, receiving more than twenty-five awards for his various acts of bravery.

You might imagine that Lt. Murphy would have worn his medals proudly, or even put them on display in his home. But this young man gave his medals away—to children. People thought he was crazy, and some no doubt thought he was unappreciative of his honors! But he felt that those awards weren't rightfully his alone, that they belonged to his whole unit. Since he didn't know how to distribute the medals among his unit, he just gave them out to children. (Story told in *Decade of Triumph: The 40s*, by Time-Life Books.) Young Lt. Murphy was a real American hero; he knew that the true value of his heroics lay in the lives that were saved, not the awards that were gained. He knew the value of the eternal over the temporal.

Your life as a new mom may seem mundane compared to Audie Murphy's life of soldiering. Everything we do, as moms, appears temporary. You feed a baby who will need feeding again in a few hours. That's temporary. You change a diaper that could need changing again in a couple of minutes! That's temporary. You comfort and rock your baby to sleep only to hear her wake up crying. It was temporary.

Yet even Audie Murphy's acts of bravery were temporary. While he may have saved lives from certain death, death would eventually claim those lives in one way or another. It was temporary. He certainly helped the Allies win World War II, but there have been other wars. Quite frankly, Audie Murphy was really just doing his job. Perhaps that, most of all, makes him a hero.

You're a hero, too, you know, when you're just doing your job. Ask your baby. She'll tell you. When you feed her, saving her from hunger, you're a hero. When you change her diaper, saving her from a terrible discomfort that she can't understand, you're a hero. When you hear her cries and come quickly, saving her from loneliness, you're a hero. When you hold her close, saving her from her own insecurity, you're a hero.

No one knows what happened to many of those medals Lt. Murphy earned. They were insignificant pieces of metal. Eternity, however, will tell us what happened to each life he saved. It will, as well, tell us what happens to the precious life you are feeding, diapering, and loving.

One day, you will tell your child about the real Hero. You'll tell her about the favorite Son, born of God's Holy Spirit and conceived in the womb of a young Jewish virgin. You'll tell your little one how this Soldier left the splendor of His heavenly home to fight for His people, and how this brave young God-Man's only medals of honor were the nail-prints in His hands and feet. Then you'll tell her that this Warrior freely gives undeserving children the award of salvation that He's earned—and guess what? Your child will understand. She'll understand the whole story because when God made her, He saw her need for the Hero, and He gave her a mom to point the way.

♥

Praise the Lord today for being your Hero.

Earning Your Stripes

"Surely he took up our infirmities
and carried our sorrows,
yet we considered him stricken by God,
smitten by him, and afflicted.
But he was pierced for our transgressions,
he was crushed for our iniquities;
the punishment that brought us peace was upon
him,
and by his wounds we are healed.
We all, like sheep, have gone astray,
each of us has turned to his own way;
and the LORD *has laid on him*
the iniquity of us all."

—Isaiah 53:4–6

I never identified more strongly with Christ and His suffering than during my childbirth experiences.

When David was born, my labor had to be induced. Because his birth was "scheduled," I arrived at the hospital after a good night's sleep, with time for a shower and even make-up. I had no worries about Danya, as my mom was at our home caring for her. Because I had been through the ordeal of childbirth before, I was confident that I knew what to expect, and I was so excited! Then something happened.

I was alone in the hospital room. Rich had gone to the business office to fill out paperwork while I changed into some lovely, drafty, institutional attire. I caught a glimpse of myself in the mirror, and suddenly, it occurred to me: the magnitude of what was about to happen and the fact that I was going to go through it alone. No one else in that hospital room would be experiencing my pain. And I didn't want to do it. I wanted the baby, but I did not want the pain. Yes, my long-term memory had finally kicked in, and it came upon me with a vengeance!

God in His sovereignty met me in that little hospital room in Paducah, Kentucky, and He comforted me with Christ's own words: *"A woman giving birth to a child has pain because her time has come; but when her baby is born she forgets the anguish because of her joy that a child is born into the world"* (John 16:21). And tearfully, I said with Christ, *"Not my will, but thine, be done"* (Luke 22:42 KJV).

Your body has changed, and so have you. Don't be distraught over stretch marks or the scar from a Cesarean. Consider it a reminder that life and breath come at a price, and eternal peace, yours and your child's, cost our Lord His very life. Just as you endured all kinds of pain willingly for the life you hold in your arms, the life that has brought you untold joy in such a short time, take comfort that Jesus, too, went to the cross just as willingly, in order to hold you, His precious child, in the everlasting arms of His love.

♥

Thank God today for His ultimate gift of salvation through Jesus Christ, His Son.

David's life verse: *"And [David] was successful in all he did, because the Lord was with him."*

—*I Samuel 18:14 TEV*

Drafted

"For you created my inmost being;
*   you knit me together in my mother's womb.*
I praise you because I am fearfully and wonderfully made;
*   your works are wonderful,*
*   I know that full well.*
My frame was not hidden from you
*   when I was made in the secret place.*
When I was woven together in the depths of the earth,
*   your eyes saw my unformed body.*
All the days ordained for me
**   were written in your book**
**   before one of them came to be."**
*   —Psalm 139:13–16*

In 1957, Elvis Presley was king. That is, he was the king of rock 'n roll, the trademark of a generation. In Elvis, teenagers saw a hero, a sex symbol, and a real-life, rags-to-riches personification of the American dream! Though he grew up in poverty, Elvis's good looks and musical talent established him as a phenomenon practically overnight. As a young man, he had it all, by the world's standards. On December 20, 1957, however, a "command performance" of sorts was issued by his Uncle Sam in the form of a draft notice. Teenage girls across the country emitted a collective moan. Not Elvis! There must be some mistake.

But there was no avoiding it. Despite his wealth and popularity, there was no escape. This was not optional. There was no choice for this young man but to answer the call and do his duty.

Do you feel as if you've been drafted and sent kicking and screaming to Baby Boot Camp? Did you consider the news of your pregnancy—the astounding discovery of another heart beating inside of you—an accident? Life is a gift from the One who breathed His life into Adam at the beginning of time. Believe it or not, I had the audacity to think that Rich and I planned our children, the timing of the pregnancies, conception, and so forth. Especially the first two. It was so easy for us, thanks be to God. With our third child, Derek, however, it was a little bit different.

We hadn't really talked about having another baby. We had a daughter and a son; what more could we want? But something was pulling at my heart to have another baby, and I was wondering about God's role in the entire family planning thing anyway. I had a lot of questions and not very many answers. I hadn't even talked to Rich about it because I felt as though I didn't have the words to explain my struggle to him. So I went to the Lord, who doesn't need our words, whose Spirit *"intercedes for us with groans that words cannot express"* (Romans 8:26b). Soon afterward, Rich came home from a men's meeting at our church, and he began relating to me what the speaker, Onnie Kirk, had talked about. Open-mouthed, I listened to Rich articulate my very burden through the words a stranger had given the men that morning. It opened up communication between Rich and me about having a third child.

But I wasn't yet willing to give up birth control. I was mostly wrestling with the concept of being pregnant for a third time: the sickness, the weight gain, the fatigue, the leg cramps. Then a few weeks later I was asked to read aloud in Sunday school from Romans 12. I stumbled on the words *"offer your bodies as living sacrifices, holy and pleasing to God—this is your spiritual act of worship."* It hit me hard. God was calling us to have another child, and I was standing in His way. Who gave me this body I was reluctant to surrender?

Derek was born about 10 months later. He's been such a joy. I'm thankful that God allowed me to see that every child is really His idea. If you didn't volunteer, if you feel as though you've been drafted, consider today's Scripture. This child is a blessing from God the Creator! He plans each life, portions out each day, and then goes ahead of us to prepare every step. Your Heavenly Father intends to make that baby a channel of His love, flowing from you to your child, and back again.

> ❤
> **Today, thank God that He has a plan for your life and that your baby is part of His plan.**

Derek's life verse: *"From birth I was cast upon you; from my mother's womb you have been my God."*
—*Psalm 22:10*

The Barracks

"And when you pray, do not be like the hypocrites, for they love to pray standing in the synagogues and on the street corners to be seen by men. I tell you the truth, they have received their reward in full. **But when you pray, go into your room, close the door and pray to your Father, who is unseen.** Then your Father, who sees what is done in secret, will reward you. And when you pray, do not keep on babbling like pagans, for they think they will be heard because of their many words. Do not be like them, for your Father knows what you need before you ask him."

—*Matthew 6:5–8*

Remember when two became one? After your husband lifted your veil, he was granted access to your body and you, as well, to his. Things changed.

Giving birth is another great transition in life, a new season. Now, two have become three! In marriage, you went from being someone's daughter to being a wife; now, because of that union, you have acquired the additional role of mother.

As a newlywed, your relationship with your husband moved to a different, deeper level when you accepted him as a part of your physical self, and you began to enjoy the fulfillment of your wedding vows. As a new mother, a metamorphosis has occurred, and once again, you have experienced it physically, spiritually, and emotionally. A relationship has changed, and this time, it's the one with your baby. The child is no longer in your womb; he's in your arms. It took some time to get used to having a husband around, and it will take time to adjust to a new baby as well.

For me, the most severe loss amid the gains has been that of my privacy. From morning after morning of interruptions during my devotional time, to always having company in the bathroom, to becoming accustomed to dressing in front of an audience, an "open door" policy has been firmly established in our home. (If you think your modesty was lost over the last nine months of doctor's visits, don't go looking for it any time soon!) But when things settle down, sister, find a quiet place, and steal away for time with the Lord. Listen to what Anne Ortlund says in her book, *Disciplines of a Beautiful Woman*:

> "When our three babies were age 2 1/2, 1 1/2, and brand new, I found my days were just one succession of bottles and diapers, and I got desperate for time with the Lord! Normally I sleep like a rock, but I said, 'Lord, if you'll help me, I'll meet with you from two to three A.M.' I kept my tryst with Him until

the schedule lightened; I didn't die; and I'm not sorry I did it. Everybody has twenty-four hours. We can soak ourselves in prayer, in His Word, in Himself, if we really want to."

Life is a series of changes. It wouldn't be any fun if it wasn't! As you acclimate to your new position as mom, you will realize your world will never be the same. But there is One who stays the same. His name is Jesus. He's the same yesterday, today, and tomorrow. Now more than ever, you need to spend time with Him daily. Establish that time alone with Him. As the world spins along, take a moment during each rotation to sit as His feet, firmly planted—and close the door.

❤

Pray today for a hunger for God's Living Word.

Holy Warrior

"Is any one of you in trouble? He should pray. Is anyone happy? Let him sing songs of praise. Is any one of you sick? He should call the elders of the church to pray over him and anoint him with oil in the name of the Lord. And the prayer offered in faith will make the sick person well; the Lord will raise him up. If he has sinned, he will be forgiven. Therefore confess your sins to each other and pray for each other so that you may be healed. **The prayer of a righteous man is powerful and effective.**

"Elijah was a man just like us. He prayed earnestly that it would not rain, and it did not rain on the land for three and a half years. Again he prayed, and the heavens gave rain, and the earth produced its crops."

—James 5:13–18

Several years ago, a popular Christian T-shirt implored, "Get on your knees and fight like a man!" The simplicity of that statement is astounding, and so true, especially when it comes to our children. How important are the prayers for your baby! Not just against sickness and SIDS—you are breathing those prayers every waking minute—but prayers for his life, the choices he'll make, his friends, his spouse, and most importantly, his salvation.

It will take time to really pray for your baby and for his future. You'll agree that there is no time better spent, but once you make a commitment to pray for that child, you'll be surprised at how difficult it is to keep. Let this fact alone motivate you to pray: the enemy knows the power of prayer. Do you?

I have found that writing down my general prayer for the kids and reading it aloud to God every day during my quiet time keeps me focused. I used the ideas in Donna Otto's book *The Stay-at-Home Mom* to develop my prayer. I've included it here as an example. (You'll notice I've included our grandchildren in the prayer as well.)

Dearest Father,
I thank you for my children. They are, indeed, a blessing from the Lord. How grateful I am for the privilege and precious responsibility of training them.

I pray for Danya, David, and Derek now, and for my grandchildren. Oh Father, sweet Abba, I pray that they will fear the Lord, and serve Him alone. May each one come to know Christ early, yet still be old enough that it creates a memory on which they can stand. May my children hate sin. I pray that these kids will be caught when they're guilty, so they may learn from their mistakes, and also, Lord, that they would be quick to confess any wrongdoing—that their hearts will be tender and inclined to repentance.

May the children have a responsible attitude toward one another and a strong sense of family loyalty. I pray they will be close and affectionate with one another. I pray that our family will respect one another and those you place in authority over us.

May the children desire the right kind of friends. Provide those friends, Lord, and protect them from the wrong kind. Save and keep them for the right spouse; please, Lord, may they and their future God-appointed spouses be pure for one another on their wedding nights.

Protect the children, Lord; please give them safety, well-being, sound minds, and good health. I pray they would never be the victims of sexual crime or perversion, or any type of violence. May they never get involved with drugs or alcohol. Protect them from wrong people and wrong places.

May the children submit to Rich and me as their parents, honoring us and loving us. May we ever strive, through Christ, to be good parents. Praying always in the name of Jesus, Amen.

As you grow into your role as mother, and change from a "holding and storage" facility to mom-cook-laundress-bather-nurse and so on, don't forget to add "soldier" to the list. You are a holy warrior, fighting for your child's abundant life!

❤

May God bless you, your husband, and
your child as you develop this most powerful
area of your parenting.

Pulling Rank

"During the fourth watch of the night Jesus went out to them, walking on the lake. When the disciples saw him walking on the lake, they were terrified. 'It's a ghost,' they said, and cried out in fear.

"But Jesus immediately said to them: 'Take courage! It is I. Don't be afraid.'

"'Lord, if it's you,' Peter replied, 'tell me to come to you on the water.'

"'Come,' he said.

"Then Peter got down out of the boat, walked on the water and came toward Jesus. But when he saw the wind, he was afraid and, beginning to sink, cried out, 'Lord, save me!'

"Immediately Jesus reached out his hand and caught him. 'You of little faith,' he said, 'why did you doubt?'

"And when they climbed into the boat, the wind died down. **Then those who were in the boat worshiped him, saying, 'Truly you are the Son of God.'**"

—Matthew 14:25–33

I've been a choir member for most of my adult life. I love it! Among the advantages are always having a seat in a crowded sanctuary and, thanks to the choir robe, not worrying if I spill a jelly doughnut on my blouse in Sunday School.

One thing I've learned from being in the choir is the importance of keeping my eyes on the director. While many talented people are responsible for leading the congregation in praise on Sunday mornings—instrumentalists, sound technicians, the praise band, and soloists as well as the choir—the choir director is the one who pulls it all together. We're supposed to take our cues from him; he's central.

Want to know the beat? *Look at the director.*

What verse are we on? *Look at the director.*

Is this in parts or unison? *Look at the director.*

In the same way, being a disciple of Christ requires that we keep our eyes on Him. There are so many distractions between here and heaven that it can get awfully confusing if we dare to give Jesus anything but our undivided attention. When He is central, life has harmony and rhythm. It's easy to dance to! But if, like Peter, we take our eyes off of Christ and look instead at the circumstances around us, we are sure to fall. Thank God, He picks us up! He lifts us out of the angry sea, and then, like Peter, we know to scoot a little closer to Him in the boat.

What about you? There are so many questions that come up with a newborn: *Bottle or breast? What about immunizations? When do we move her to the crib? Cloth diapers or disposables?* Your favorite baby book is telling you one thing; your mother is telling you another. Your mom-in-law is telling your husband what you should do. Your friends are telling you what they did, and you feel overwhelmed, confused, and even a little ticked off. It happens. People are just trying to help. They do have the best intentions, really, but remember, this is *your* baby, Mom. You and she were made for each other, by God's great design. Don't let anyone pull rank on you just because you're new at all this. You have a wonderful mother's instinct that was created within you when you gave birth to that child. You know, deep down, what is best for that baby. And when you don't know, just ask the Lord. He'll provide wise counsel, if you just ask Him. He's the director. His rhythm is steady. His melody is sweet.

Keep your eyes on Him.

❤
**Ask God today to help you
keep your eyes on Jesus.**

At Ease

"You who bring good tidings to Zion,
go up on a high mountain.
You who bring good tidings to Jerusalem,
lift up your voice with a shout,
lift it up, do not be afraid;
say to the towns of Judah,
'Here is your God!'
See, the Sovereign LORD comes with power,
and his arm rules for him.
See, his reward is with him,
and his recompense accompanies him.
He tends his flock like a shepherd:
He gathers the lambs in his arms
and carries them close to his heart;
 he gently leads those that have young."
 —Isaiah 40:9–11

Have you ever watched a movie or television show with a military plot and noticed the stress of the moment when a commanding officer confronts enlisted men? A sergeant shouts, "A-TEN-SHUN!" and the platoon immediately assumes the stiff, practiced stance. Following is a moment of nervous hesitation, until the ranking officer nods, "At ease!" A play on words could easily be made between the moment of "at *tension*" and "at ease."

Your contractions during the birth process were a series of moments "at tension" and "at ease." During the contraction, you rode a wave of searing pain, and between each one, you were utterly amazed at the absence of that agony. The difference was like night and day. You knew when to rest, and you knew when to push, simply by following the rhythms of your body. And it was tolerable because you knew what you were working for. Your eyes were on the prize, the finish line, the moment you would hold that baby for the first time.

Pain and purpose are inexplicably bound in the Bible. There is no needless suffering. It has a purpose. God has a plan, whether we understand it or not. The heart of our loving Lord lies in the fact that while sin increased the pain of labor (see Genesis 3:16), He equipped us with an endowment of endurance. He enabled us with a little R&R in the middle of the war! Truly, He is the Gentle Shepherd. He desires to share His lovingkindness with us and with our children.

So don't be so hard on yourself—don't try to do it all. You simply can't. And believe it or not, no one expects you to. Follow His gentle leading. Accept the help offered you by your husband, your parents, your in-laws, and your friends. Bless your loved ones by allowing them the gift of service.

Maybe you're pushing yourself now, when you should be resting. "Sleep when the baby sleeps," is great advice for a new mom. Ask yourself, honestly, *What needs to be done? What can wait? What can my husband or the baby's grandmother do?* Perhaps you're worrying needlessly over a temporary situation. Focus on the picture Isaiah's words create: our Gentle Shepherd, Jesus, who carries us close in His arms, close to His heart, tenderly leads us mothers and our little ones.

At ease, Mom. At ease.

❤

Praise God today for His gentle ways of mercy.

Battle Fatigue

"Your attitude should be the same as that of Christ Jesus:
Who, being in very nature God,
  did not consider equality with God something to be grasped,
but made himself nothing,
  taking the very nature of a servant,
  being made in human likeness.
And being found in appearance as a man,
  he humbled himself
  and became obedient to death—even death on a cross!
Therefore God exalted him to the highest place
  and gave him the name that is above every name,
that at the name of Jesus every knee should bow,
  in heaven and on earth and under the earth,
and every tongue confess that Jesus Christ is Lord,
  to the glory of God the Father."
—Philippians 2:5–11

God's Word gives a detailed explanation of the most awesome rescue ever attempted: saving a dying world from its sin-sick self through the blood of the Holy Son of God. There was no other way for God to draw His own creation unto Himself, separated as we were from His holiness by our own free will. So the Father sent His Son to bridge the gap, to be the link, to bind together God and man. In Philippians 2, Christ's obedience is beautifully illustrated in the text: God became man. He took on a body of flesh with all its weaknesses and limitations.

There is nothing quite like childbirth to cause a woman to realize just how fearfully and wonderfully her body is made. It is also, combined with the extreme fatigue in the weeks that follow, a time to admit how weak and limited her flesh is. Your body needs time to recover from all it has spent on growing the life you now hold and continue to nourish. Getting only patches of sleep night after night continues to deplete your resources. Truly, it is only temporary, my sister. That baby will sleep through the night soon, the two of you will develop a feeding schedule that works, and your energy will return.

I remember being at my most desperate during those first six weeks with Danya. My sons nursed more frequently through the night, but both of them settled back down pretty easily. Danya was a different story. She was up at night because she was unhappy, and while I spent that time praying for her *(Lord, please, show me what to do! Tell me what's wrong with her. Make her stop crying and go back to sleep!)*, the worst part of it, besides being worn out, was the loneliness. (Rich had to be the one to sleep because he was the one going to work the next day. He always helped on the weekends.) Satan can play games with your mind, especially when your body is weak.

Focus not on your weaknesses or limitations but on Christ. Remember Gethsemane when you find yourself awake and praying during the lonely hours of the night, when you feel like the world has turned upside-down, when you're overwhelmed, when you're depressed and afraid. Jesus Christ has been there. He understands loneliness and doubt and fear. But He overcame all that, and He offers you His victory. If you are experiencing battle fatigue, remember: the war has been won.

♥

**Thank God today for the victory
that is yours in Christ Jesus.**

Humor Under Fire

"Jesus withdrew to the region of Tyre and Sidon. A Canaanite woman from that vicinity came to him, crying out, 'Lord, Son of David, have mercy on me! My daughter is suffering terribly from demon-possession.'

"Jesus did not answer a word. So his disciples came to him and urged him, 'Send her away, for she keeps crying out after us.'

"He answered, 'I was sent only to the lost sheep of Israel.'

"The woman came and knelt before him. 'Lord, help me!' she said.

"He replied, 'It is not right to take the children's bread and toss it to their dogs.'

"'Yes, Lord,' she said, 'but even the dogs eat the crumbs that fall from their masters' table.'

"Then Jesus answered, 'Woman you have great faith! Your request is granted.' *And her daughter was healed from that very hour."*

—Matthew 15:21–28

In the Scripture above, a woman has come to Jesus begging for the healing of her daughter, who is demon-possessed. (Sound familiar? That was you last night, begging for that colicky baby to calm down and go to sleep!) Strangely enough, she appears to be ignored by the loving Savior. (Isn't that how you felt, too?) And then the Lord tests her faith by asserting that He was "sent only to the lost sheep of Israel." (Don't you see? This is only a test!) So the woman falls down before Him, aligning herself with the Jews by professing Him as Lord. (Did it occur to you to do that? My friend Tera got that far with her son, Alex. "Lord," she called out desperately after a week of sleepless nights, "You are the God of Abraham, Isaac, and Jacob. You parted the Red Sea for the deliverance of Your people, Israel. Won't You please, please, make this baby hush and go to sleep?")

Yet even after the woman's profession, Jesus seemingly refuses her request. "It is not right to take the children's bread and toss it to the dogs" (verse 26). A moment before, she had declared her faith in Christ.

Was it all lip service?

Would she get mad and walk away after Christ's response?

Would she give up in tears and decide He wasn't who she thought He was?

No way!

She answered with great courage and even greater wit: "Even the dogs eat the crumbs that fall from their master's table." She wasn't arguing; in fact, I'd go so far as to say, with all due respect, it was an even-handed verbal exchange. She knew who He was, and indeed, she had made Him her Lord; so she came boldly to the throne. As an intimate friend, she made her needs known.

I wish I could have witnessed this Canaanite mom bantering with the Creator of the universe. Initially, she came to this young Jewish man desperately pleading for her daughter's sanity. The disciples considered her a pest. But once she began professing her faith and proclaiming the identity of Christ, her confidence in Him was established. I believe she pleased the Lord with her wit, her outspokenness, and the honest approach of her petition.

Bible scholars may disagree, but I think the Lord must have grinned at her comeback, appreciating her humor under fire. He healed her daughter because of her faith, right? When her faith was tested, she responded with *more* faith and a sense of humor. We would do well to mimic this mother.

There is more humor on the other side of these first six weeks than there is in the midst of them, for both you and your child. It's hard to laugh when you're up night after night, feeling like a human pacifier. There's nothing funny about colic, or ear infections, or that total feeling of inadequacy that occurs once you realize the monumental task that you have begun in motherhood.

Perhaps you are longing for a deeper relationship with this Christ. He knows you need Him now, more than ever. Have you been coming to Him desperately, especially when you are so exhausted from all the new demands on your body, mind, and soul?

He is not ignoring you. He loves you. You are made in His image, and so is your baby. Be confident, then, for this is only a test.

❤

**Profess your faith in Him today,
and proclaim His identity!**

About-Face

"I rejoice greatly in the Lord that at last you have renewed your concern for me. Indeed, you have been concerned, but you had no opportunity to show it. I am not saying this because I am in need, for I have learned to be content whatever the circumstances. I know what it is to be in need, and I know what it is to have plenty. **I have learned the secret of being content in any and every situation, whether well fed or hungry, whether living in plenty or in want. I can do everything through him who gives me strength.**"

—*Philippians 4:10–13*

My friend Donna had a really sweet baby girl named Liza [both names have been changed]. At about six months old, Liza loved to go places with her mom. She was content on short trips in her car seat. When she did fuss, she was easily pacified with objects from Donna's purse: pictures, a comb, or sunglasses. One of her favorite "toys" was Donna's lipstick case. Liza had never opened it and discovered the lipstick inside; she just loved holding the case.

One evening, when Donna's husband was working late, her parents invited Donna and the baby to meet them for dinner at a nearby cafeteria. Rush hour traffic was heavy. When it came to a complete stop, Liza began to get restless. Donna passed her lipstick case back to her to play with. Ahead she saw flashing blue lights and a couple of police cars. As they inched past the accident causing the delay, an ambulance came through. Donna began praying for the people who had been hurt. She became concerned in her own thoughts about the accident, and she began to worry: *What if that had been me? What if I had a wreck, and something happened to Liza?* When she finally pulled up at the cafeteria, she had tears in her eyes from her own dramatic imaginings. By then, dusk had turned to dark, and when she went to get the baby out of her car seat, Donna screamed in horror. Liza was covered in blood! Donna's screams turned into great sobs, and her parents, who had been watching for her, ran out to see what was wrong.

"What happened?"

"I don't know! Liza's been hurt! She's bleeding!"

By this time, Liza had joined in her mother's panic, and she was crying, too. They rushed inside. Once in the well-lit restaurant Donna abruptly stopped crying.

"Oh," she said rather meekly. "It's lipstick." Everyone's emotions did a quick about-face as Donna began to laugh and held up the opened lipstick that Liza had been clutching in her "bloody" little fist. "It's my lipstick! She finally figured out how to open it!"

Donna had forgotten giving Liza that lipstick case. Sometimes I, too, get so engrossed in situations around me that I forget what I'm doing. I lose my focus. My vision gets skewed in the dim light, and I have to draw near to God, getting back to the Light, to see what's really going on. It's those times when we cannot see clearly that we rely most on our faith.

Ron Griffith is a career military man, a four-star general. He served in Vietnam and the Gulf War. He said in an article in *New Man* magazine (July/August 1997), "In combat there was a keen awareness that every day you were subject to not getting through the day, which causes you to think a great deal about your faith."

During my first weeks with a new baby, and even now, living with three kids, there are days when I truly feel like I'm in combat—and I'm losing! Usually when that happens, I'm looking at my circumstances, and I'm overwhelmed with all that needs to be done. Discipleship must not depend on our life's circumstances. The apostle Paul was severely persecuted, and yet he persevered in his Christian walk. General Griffith says, "I am not a spiritual giant. But I am a true believer. I certainly have great faith. All of us have challenges to face— illness, disabilities, burdens, children with problems. Faith is what gets you through. It gives you calm when there is no reason to be calm. Faith is an absolute fact in my life, and I believe it applies to anybody who wants to draw upon it."

When you feel like you are swinging on that

pendulum between blood and lipstick, the secret to finding your balance is not in the latest Dobson book, or in calling your mother, or in a pack of M&Ms. It's in Christ.

♥

**Thank God that upon close inspection,
life's blood is often just lipstick!**

Camouflaged

"Likewise, teach the older women to be reverent in the way they live, not to be slanderers or addicted to much wine, but to teach what is good. **Then they can train the younger women to love their husbands and children,** *to be self-controlled and pure, to be busy at home, to be kind, and to be subject to their husbands, so that no one will malign the word of God."*

—*Titus 2:3–5*

An attractive young mother announced with despair to her Sunday school class, "I just can't do it. And I don't understand how any of you can!" Tearfully, she went on to express her frustration with the demands of raising two children under two years of age. She felt isolated during the week, watching her husband and neighbors leave for work while she was at home all day with the babies. She brought a torrent of emotions with her to church every Sunday morning, only to leave after services with her burden still intact. You see, she came to church seeking solace and understanding from other women, only to find—amid the masks of carefully made-up, dressed-up Christians—not one hair out of place, and children being cared for in the nursery. That's not reality, but that is Sunday morning.

Fortunately, when my first baby came along I had Kathy Fletcher in my life, and therefore I had a totally different perspective on how other moms "did it." Kathy was a few years older than I was, and her daughter Katelyn was about 15 months old when Danya was born. Kathy invited me for lunch when her house didn't look perfect, she didn't look perfect, and Katelyn didn't look perfect. The first time she had me over, she was showing me around her house, and she stopped to explain her "piles."

"These are my piles," she said with a laugh as she pointed to boxes of clothes she was sorting through and various stacks of papers in the middle of what should have been her formal living room. "It sounds like a disease. My piles! I can't keep it all straight right now, but I know I'll be able to clean my house all day long when Katelyn's grown and gone." She really lived that way. Kathy always had time to talk and to pray and to laugh over Cheerios crunching under our shoes on the kitchen floor. What a blessing for a new mom from a seasoned one: learning the priority of the eternal over the temporary. That squalling babe who wants to nurse every two hours and most of the night will one day be pouring juice for your grandchildren. Between now and then, what's important?

Like every child, Katelyn didn't always behave

perfectly. When Katelyn misbehaved, Kathy disciplined her right in front of me, showing a loving firmness that wouldn't wait until company left or until Daddy got home, giving me a pattern to follow when my own child reached those "terrific twos." Don't get me wrong—she was always careful not to embarrass Katelyn. Sometimes they had to leave the room for a more intense reprimand. From Kathy I learned how time-out, spanking, and stickers on a chart could all work together beautifully. I also learned that teaching a preschooler the proper way to behave ranks higher than making sure your guest gets her tea glass refilled. Kathy was always a mom first and hostess second. I gained much from seeing her practice consistency with her child.

I was on my own with my first baby, living miles away from both my mom and my mother-in-law. Kathy and I had begun teaching the three-year-olds at church, and once a week we got together at her place for our planning time. God provided greatly for me through her Christian example of mothering.

My prayers are with you, new mom, as you just live through the first year and do the best you can. It does get easier. It helps to remember that you are not alone! Hook up with a mom you think of not as perfect, but as real. After all, most of those Sunday morning moms were up half the night, fussed with their husbands that morning, yelled at the kids in the car on the way to church, and then glued on their masks as camouflage when they walked in the door.

♥

Pray today for the courage to be a real mom.

Unsung Hero

"When Jesus looked up and saw a great crowd coming toward him, he said to Philip, 'Where shall we buy bread for these people to eat?' He asked this only to test him, for he already had in mind what he was going to do.

"Philip answered him, 'Eight months' wages would not buy enough bread for each one to have a bite!'

"Another of his disciples, Andrew, Simon Peter's brother, spoke up, 'Here is a boy with five small barley loaves and two small fish, but how far will they go among so many?'

"Jesus said, 'Have the people sit down.' There was plenty of grass in that place, and the men sat down, about five thousand of them. Jesus then took the loaves, gave thanks, and distributed to those who were seated as much as they wanted. He did the same with the fish.

"When they had all had enough to eat, he said to his disciples, 'Gather the pieces that are left over. Let nothing be wasted.' So they gathered them and filled twelve baskets with the pieces of the five barley loaves left over by those who had eaten."

—John 6:5–13

What a familiar story, that of the little boy who shared his lunch with Jesus. Jesus took that tiny offering and multiplied it into the miraculous feast that fed over five thousand people. Maybe you first heard that story as a child. It is often used in children's Sunday school lessons as an illustration of what can happen when a person chooses to share with others. Many points can be drawn as well from looking at what happens when we give whatever we have, great or small, to Jesus.

Now, however, you're a mother. Perhaps it's time to look at God's Word from that perspective and speculate that there must be a mother involved in this story. We will never have concrete evidence of her this side of heaven, but I know deep in my heart that she existed.

She rose early that morning to pack a lunch for her son. She had heard that Jesus would be nearby that day, and she knew many people were going to listen to His teachings. Yet she was caring for aging parents, or she had a new baby, or she just simply had too much to do—she couldn't get away. Instead, she encouraged her son to go and listen to the young teacher. As she handed him the lunch sack, she may have said, "Listen carefully, and remember everything that happens, so you can tell me all about it when you get home." Then she went about her day, busy with all the routine chores that are never truly appreciated, but sorely missed when left undone.

When the boy arrived home that night, he told that precious mother what Jesus had done with his lunch. Can you imagine? First, the pride she felt in her child for his generosity, and then, the realization that she had unknowingly packed a banquet in a bag! Though she is never mentioned in the Scripture, she is an important part of that feast, that miracle on the hill.

As you settle into a routine with your baby, you may become frustrated with the monotony of this postpartum life behind the scenes. After all, anybody can change diapers, and rock, and wash twenty-five pounds of laundry a week. Anybody could have packed that lunch. But God chose her. And God chose you. Together, you are enlisted in the ranks of moms who are the unsung heroes of our American culture. As you bless your child with your faithfulness, God will bless you with His faithfulness, and nothing will be wasted.

❤

Thank God today for choosing you.

Green Berets

"Again the Israelites did evil in the eyes of the LORD, so the LORD delivered them into the hands of the Philistines for forty years.

"A certain man of Zorah, named Manoah, from the clan of the Danites, had a wife who was sterile and remained childless. The angel of the LORD appeared to her and said, 'You are sterile and childless, but you are going to conceive and have a son. Now see to it that you drink no wine or other fermented drink and that you do not eat anything unclean, because you will conceive and give birth to a son. No razor may be used on his head, because the boy is to be a Nazirite, **set apart to God from birth,** and he will begin the deliverance of Israel from the hands of the Philistines.'

"Then the woman went to her husband and told him, 'A man of God came to me. He looked like an angel of God, very awesome. I didn't ask him where he came from, and he didn't tell me his name. But he said to me, "You will conceive and give birth to a son. Now then, drink no wine or other fermented drink and do not eat anything unclean, because the boy will be a Nazirite of God from birth until the day of his death."'

"Then Manoah prayed to the LORD: 'O Lord, I beg you, let the man of God you sent to us come again to teach us how to bring up the boy who is to be born.'"
—*Judges 13:1–8*

The U.S. Army Special Forces personnel are known for their exceptional training in survival techniques, communication skills, weaponry, and even parachuting. Most often called upon to infiltrate behind enemy lines, these people are also known for the green berets that are part of their uniforms. The green berets set them apart, distinguishing them as members of that highly-trained unit.

Each one of us is "set apart" from birth, as God has a plan for each life. Because of the gift of free will, it is up to each individual to decide whether or not she follows God's plan for her life. Sometimes, God blesses families with children that are "set apart" by certain needs or talents. Samson's mother was told by an angel that her yet-to-be-conceived child had been appointed by God to *"begin the deliverance of Israel from the hands of the Philistines"* (verse 5). Mothers today may be told of the notable features of their unborn children by way of a sonogram or amniocentesis. Whether or not you were told of a special need before your baby arrived or months later find you're living with a genius, all of us can say with Manoah, Samson's dad: *"O Lord, I beg you . . . teach us how to bring up the [child] who is to be born"* (verse 8).

On a late summer evening in 1994, I was watching the Miss America Pageant with my sister. We had missed the first part of the broadcast but tuned in just in time to see a lovely young woman doing a ballet routine to the Christian song "Via Dolorosa." I was thrilled to see a contestant sharing her Christian faith in such a bold way and rejoiced in her witness for Christ. Her performance was beautiful. As the show progressed from talent to interview, I was astounded to learn this dancer was deaf. Her name was Heather Whitestone, and that night she was crowned Miss America.

Her mother, Daphne Gray, has written Heather's incredible story in *Yes, You Can, Heather!* It is the story of a daughter, a mom, and the struggle they shared. It is also the story of a God who sees us through whatever life brings. We can all learn from Daphne's candid account of the anger she felt upon the discovery that Heather was profoundly deaf. Daphne is a real mom—no mask here. She was mad at God. She says in her book, "The funny thing was, as angry as I became with God, I found I couldn't quit talking to Him altogether. I guess old habits die hard. Because even during my angriest times, when I'd feel the most frustrated, frightened, or helpless, I'd catch myself inadvertently calling out to Him for help and guidance."

God didn't leave Daphne. He heard her, just as He heard Manoah's prayer, just as He hears you. All children are special, but some arrive with special needs, and they depend on us in a way for which we feel totally unprepared. I want to tell you that even as the Green Berets receive the most specialized training for their assignments, so God will teach and train you for a customized fit with the child He gives you to parent.

Daphne also writes about the day she had taken Heather and her two sisters to play at a local park. She was enjoying watching her daughters interact with other children and admiring the loving way the older girls had learned to treat Heather naturally, yet still allow for her deafness. Daphne writes, "In that moment, God seemed to speak directly to my heart. 'You're seeing what needs to be done. You're seeing what Heather can do, how she can fit in.

"'Enough with the self-pity! It's time for you to quit feeling sorry for yourself! You can sit there being angry forever, but that won't do you any good. And it won't help Heather or those two other little girls. It's time to get up and move on. There are decisions to be made. I've been with you. I'm here with you now. And I'll be there to help you and guide you all the way. You just have to trust me.'"

♥

Pray today for a heart surrendered to the Savior, trusting Him for now and for eternity, and for every moment in between.

The Battle of the Bulge

"The Spirit clearly says that in later times some will abandon the faith and follow deceiving spirits and things taught by demons. Such teachings come through hypocritical liars, whose consciences have been seared as with a hot iron. They forbid people to marry and order them to abstain from certain foods, which God created to be received with thanksgiving by those who believe and who know the truth. For everything God created is good, and nothing is to be rejected if it is received with thanksgiving, because it is consecrated by the word of God and prayer.

*"If you point these things out to the brothers, you will be a good minister of Christ Jesus, brought up in the truths of the faith and of the good teaching that you have followed. Have nothing to do with godless myths and old wives' tales; rather, train yourself to be godly. **For physical training is of some value, but godliness has value for all things, holding promise for both the present life and the life to come."***

—I Timothy 4:1–8

Did you know that there actually was a real-life Battle of the Bulge? It occurred during the second World War, lasting for six bloody weeks with great casualties on both sides. They called it the Battle of the Bulge because of the bulging shape of the battleground area as seen on a military map. The Allied forces almost lost this one, and at one point, the German ground commander asked for their surrender. Allied Forces Brig. Gen. Anthony C. McAuliffe replied, "Nuts." Within a few weeks the Allies had recovered all ground lost in battle and trapped more than 300,000 enemy soldiers. Our contemporary use of a "battle of the bulge" is to describe people's personal struggles with body weight. I certainly hope this is not an issue with you, but if it is, read on.

Moments after I delivered Danya, the O.B. nurse took my hand and said gently, "You remember, it took you nine months to gain your baby weight. Give yourself nine months to get it off." I said with the good Brig. Gen. McAuliffe, "Nuts." It has been my personal experience, and well-documented by the medical profession, that the longer that weight stays on you, *the longer it stays on you!*

Breast-feeding helps to get it off, but so does your own common sense. If you've never been at home full-time before, you may be thankful you are miles away from tempting vending machines—but beware, if you load up on goodies at the grocery store, you're asking for trouble. Try to keep it out of the house.

You will need more calories now, but as you may have read in the *What to Expect* books, make sure those calories count. No empty calories, but get those extra calories from foods rich in protein. When your doctor gives you the go-ahead, return to your exercise program or get started with one. Put that new stroller to use and go walking. Babies love to stroll—through your neighborhood, at the mall (avoid the food court), and at a nearby park. You can do it!

More important than your physical training, as Paul told Timothy in today's Scripture, is your spiritual training. Are you filling up on empty calories? Think about the choices you are making regarding what you watch, read, and listen to. You are not home alone. Do your habits reflect those of a person who is spending her day with Jesus Christ, modeling His likeness for her new baby?

I confess when I began staying at home I had a favorite soap opera that I had started watching at work. It aired during my lunchtime, and my boss and I would watch it together in the breakroom. I got to put my feet up for an hour, chat with my sweet boss, and keep myself busy by making excuses for why it was okay that I was watching these people on television break all 10 commandments every 20 minutes and call it entertainment.

It doesn't take long for Satan to spot an area in your life where he can gain a foothold. I was ripe. Once Danya was born, my famous excuse of "I'll stop watching this when I'm at home" turned into "This is the only time I get to sit down." I was hooked. I was under conviction, too. I realized this was five hours a week of wasted time—valuable time, time that could be much better spent. Why was it so much easier to turn on the TV instead of to pick up my Bible? When I began dreaming about the characters in the program, I knew it was out of my control. It was way past time to give it up to the Lord, and so I finally did. It wasn't easy, and I was sorely tempted in the beginning, but the Lord helped me to turn it off, keep it off, and not look back.

God alone can give you the discipline to avoid empty calories in your life, both spiritual and physical. I know He can. He's done it for me.

♥

**Ask the Great Physician today
if He has a diet and exercise program for you.**

Target Practice

"The rod of correction imparts wisdom,
  but a child left to himself disgraces his mother.
When the wicked thrive, so does sin,
  but the righteous will see their downfall.
Discipline your son, and he will give you peace;
  he will bring delight to your soul.
Where there is no revelation, the people cast off restraint;
  but blessed is he who keeps the law."
—Proverbs 29:15–18

How did the struggling colonists overcome the established nation of England in the Revolutionary War? They had not the financial means, nor the weaponry, nor the supplies of their former homeland. What our forebears did have, however, was a vision of a free country. Although they could not see the future, they could dream of it. They set their goals, determined their objectives, counted the costs, and then they didn't quit. There were many setbacks, but the American spirit could not be extinguished. These fearless, faithful fighters stood firm. Today, though I'll be the first to admit we have many problems, America is still the superpower and still the greatest land on earth.

What is your vision for your child? One day, that totally dependent newborn will be an independent adult. Since businesses have productivity goals, five- and ten-year plans, and financial forecasts, why shouldn't we mothers do the same in our business of raising godly kids? What are your goals in child rearing? What character traits do you long to see in your children when they are grown? When you envision the finished product 18 years down the road, what do you hope for?

A few years ago, I sat down with pen and paper and came before the Lord requesting that He show me what my vision for my children should be. The following is the result of that prayer:

My vision for my children is that they become mature Christians: leading godly lives, holding the Bible as the standard by which all else is measured, capable of offering wise counsel to others, and totally accountable to God for their whole conduct and every thought.

My prayer is that each one chooses submission to the Lord over his or her selfish will and that they would enjoy abundant life through a close, personal relationship with the living Christ, loving Him with all of their hearts, minds, and souls. May these children be "pillars of the church, soldiers of the cross, and true

servants of Jesus."* This I pray in that blessed,
wonderful name of Jesus, Amen.

* This quote is from Luis Palau's prayer for his sons (*New Man* magazine, June 1997).

I try to bring this petition before the Lord every morning. I find it helps in establishing my priorities, the eternal over the temporal, as I face each day at home with my children. Anne Ortlund says in *Disciplines of a Beautiful Woman*, "You know, the longer I live, the more I realize that all that's important in this life is God, and people, and connecting the former with the latter. I'm willing to shed a lot of things to strive after the Important."

What about you, Mom? It's normal at this point of postpartum to be ready to pull yourself together, clean the house, and set up a routine. All of that is positive and good, but "getting back to normal" is not your immediate or your everlasting goal. You hold in your arms a baby. He doesn't care if the house is picked-up or if you have your make-up on. Unfortunately, he doesn't seem to be concerned that your breasts are sore and you are exhausted. All he wants to know is that if he cries, you're there. While you may be aiming for him to sleep through the night and, of course, you are shooting for developing a nursing or feeding schedule that works for both of you, the bull's eye of this target is centered in the fact that you are this child's connection to Christ, who is his connection to God. Remembering that, everything else will line up with a godly perspective and patience you have never before experienced. Really!

❤

Pray that during today's target practice, you don't run out of ammunition!

In Triplicate

"The LORD spoke to Moses in the Tent of Meeting in the Desert of Sinai on the first day of the second month of the second year after the Israelites came out of Egypt. He said: *'Take a census of the whole Israelite community by their clans and families, listing every man by name, one by one.* You and Aaron are to number by their divisions all the men in Israel twenty years old or more who are able to serve in the army. One man from each tribe, each the head of his family, is to help you.'"

—Numbers 1:1–4

The Book of Numbers reveals God's great love for us in a special way by drawing attention to His eye for details. We may be quite familiar with the verse that tells us every hair on our heads is numbered, but did you ever stop to think about it? Many times, in wading through lists of names, lineages, and facts in the Old Testament, I'll admit I have been prone to skim through them or skip them altogether. But they, just as everything else in God's

Word, are there for a reason.

Our God is a God of order, not chaos.

Unity, not division.

Sanity, not lunacy.

Thank God for Moses' obedience to Him. The first step in developing the nation of Israel was to organize it. A census, including names and lists and numbers, had to be taken. God cared for His people. Each one was special. They were truly His "treasured possession" (Deuteronomy 26:18), and He wanted them to know it, not by cleaning their tents and airing out their sleeping mats, but by recording their names, one by one.

What does your home look like today? Is it in a total shambles? A baby swing and a playpen are in the living room. An infant seat is on the kitchen table. The dishwasher and the sink are full. The refrigerator is empty. The laundry basket is overflowing, and what else? Dust an inch thick and floors that long to be vacuumed! Guess what? I believe that your home organization will come later, not in the first six weeks. You'll get to it. But there is something you can do today that will show your baby you love him more than a clean house.

Of course you are keeping your baby book up-to-date (I hope!), but in addition to that, try filling a Ziploc bag with the outfit your baby wore home from the hospital, a picture, the identification bracelets you both wore, and a letter from you. You might want to mention in your letter what the baby's name means, why it was chosen, and how well it fits him. Put it in a safe place, and know that you have done something special for your child. Be sure that you do this for all your babies, one by one. (That means I've done it in triplicate!) That baby book, while filled with every detail of your first one, often gets ignored with subsequent children. Even if you never fill out that baby book, do this today, and in years to come you will still have something to look at and share with your child. Who knows, you may even hold a grandbaby clothed in that special garment! My mother saved a little blue dress of mine, and she gave it to me for Danya to wear. It was so special knowing that Mom had saved that dress all those years, giving me something from my baby days to share with my own baby.

You may be thinking that you really don't have time to do this today, but remember that tomorrow, like today, holds no more than 24 hours. Take time to do this! You'll be glad you did.

❤
Thank God for His order amid our chaos.

Day 22

Military Secrets
Sound Advice from Sane Mothers

*"Trust in the L*ord* with all your heart*
  *and **lean not on your own understanding;***
in all your ways acknowledge him,
  and he will make your paths straight."
                              —*Proverbs 3:5–6*

At my first baby shower, given by my Sunday school class in Charlotte, North Carolina, I received a little booklet made up of the other moms' best mothering advice. It is a treasure that I look forward to sharing with Danya some day. I'm happy to pass along the best of their wisdom, as well as more tips I've picked up from moms along the way.

Kathy's Sheet Trick
When making up the crib, start with a fitted sheet, then add a crib-size waterproof pad, then finish with another fitted sheet. If Baby spits up or vomits in the bed, just take off the top two layers (sheet and

pad), and you are ready to settle her down again. (This beats hunting for clean crib sheets at 2:00 A.M.)

Vicki's Changing Stations
If you have a two-story house, be sure to have a diaper changing station on each floor. Vicki had her son Carson's changing table in his upstairs bedroom, where she kept all her diaper-changing supplies. Since Vicki has a bad back, it didn't take long for her to realize the benefits of that changing table and the disadvantage of having to go upstairs every time she needed to change a diaper. She set up another changing station in her kitchen, with a pack of diapers and supplies stored in a cabinet, using the top of her island for changes. (After we realized what Vicki was using her kitchen island for, we ate only take-out with them until Carson was potty-trained.)

Eric's 7:00 P.M. Feeding
When Katelyn was born, Kathy had made the decision to nurse, and it was working out beautifully. But when Katelyn turned three months old, Kathy had a brilliant idea of how to let her husband Eric share the feeding time, too. The age of three months is the ideal time to introduce a bottle for supplemental feedings. Kathy let Eric be the one to introduce Katelyn to the bottle, and she chose 7:00 P.M. as their time together. This let Eric wind down from a busy day and enjoy his baby. It gave Kathy a well-deserved break, also giving her a night out occasionally for friends or for meetings at church.

Yvonne's Kiss and Tell Philosophy

1. Pray and read the Bible the first quiet moment you get each day.
2. Get lots of advice, but trust your "mother's instincts." You know that baby better than anyone.
3. Take loads of pictures.
4. Kiss that baby constantly.
5. Kiss your husband more!

Sherry on Fragility

Children aren't as fragile as we think. They are flexible—even more so than we are. Give them the freedom to self-discover and explore their world without our apprehension.

Loretta on Life as a Human Pacifier

If you nurse, be prepared to feel some days that all you're doing is nursing. It's okay; babies do grow fast, and you won't be able to hold them for long.

Lorie's Coleslaw Recipe

You may become engorged during the first days of nursing and later, too, as the baby's needs or schedule changes. When this happens, try putting a leaf of red cabbage on each side of your bra. This will reduce the swelling! When the leaf wilts, simply replace it with a fresh one until you feel comfortable again.

Micca's Emergency Number

When the going gets tough, call your mother!

Debbie with Profound and Practical Advice
Profound: Mothering is summed up in 1 Corinthians 13. If you live by this as you interact with your baby, you cannot go wrong!
Practical: When starting to nurse, be patient, nurse often, drink lots of water, and rest!

Marla with a Word for Dad
Although it may be difficult at first, take time for you and your husband.

Rebecca's Best Baby Bottoms
Smear the white diaper cream (Desitin or discount brand) all over baby's bottom every night when you make the last diaper change. I have raised three spotless bottoms proving that an ounce of prevention is worth a pound of cure! (It's also a good idea to use it more frequently when baby is on an antibiotic medicine, especially for baby girls.)

The Last Word from Kathy
When folks give you advice (and they will), smile politely, listen, and *do what you think is right!*

❤

Pray today that God will surround you with wise counsel.

The Colonel

*"Love is patient, love is kind. It does not envy, it does not boast, it is not proud. It is not rude, it is not self-seeking, it is not easily angered, it keeps no record of wrongs. Love does not delight in evil but rejoices with the truth. It always protects, always trusts, always hopes, always perseveres. Love never fails. . . . And now these three remain: faith, hope and love. **But the greatest of these is love.**"*

—1 Corinthians 13:4–8a, 13

When I was pregnant with my first baby, it surprised me how many of the girls in my Lamaze class had deep-seated fears about raising their babies. I was too busy concentrating on keeping my food down, keeping my blood pressure down, and keeping my feet up to have even considered for a moment that I couldn't do the "mom" thing. I had a great mom, I reasoned, so following her example, I should be able to turn out a ton of kids as great as I am!

But when my kids came along, I realized that

our loving God provided that our memories don't really kick in until age three. (He provided this for our mothers, so we don't remember all their mistakes. Thankfully, it works for us now.) I had no idea how my mother had raised us girls when we were preschoolers—I only knew it could be nothing like the way she was treating her grandkids. So I was going to be winging it for the early years with my children. Then one day I sat down and did my best to think of my earliest recollections of my mom. Maybe you would want to try this, too. Here's what I came up with:

I remember being very, very sick and my mom rocking me in the middle of the night. I remember how close we were and how glad I was to hang on to her. Her robe felt so soft, and the house was still, except that rocking chair, back and forth. More than any feeling of sickness, I remember a feeling of security. Relief, even. I might have been sick, but I was safe.

One morning when I must have been around four (and it must have been one of "those" mornings because I remember this crazy, flustered feeling of haste), my mom came rushing into my room, ready to leave for school. She taught morning kindergarten then at a nearby church school while I was in preschool down the hall. Since I was already dressing myself at this age, Mom asked me if I had put on my slip. I was notorious (even in those days) for not wearing my petticoat. I remember vividly how I began to back toward the wall as, nodding, I said, "Yes."

It mattered not that we were in a hurry. My

mom didn't overlook a lie. Since my slip was still in my drawer, and she could see that I was fibbing, she spanked my bottom, lifted off my dress, put the slip on me, the dress back on, then my coat, and we were off. (I'll bet we got there right on time.) I never could lie to my mom, thank God, and she was never one to overlook discipline for the sake of convenience.

My fondest early memory of my mother lacks details. All I remember is that we were talking about something, and I responded, "Thank you, but no thank you." My mom looked at me with a look that said she thought I was the cutest, funniest person alive. It was in her eyes and all over her face. With laughter, she pulled me close to her and said, "I love you!" And I knew she really did. This woman that I adored, adored me too. I knew it was real. That, too, must have happened when I was just a preschooler, but I still remember it, and I still know it's true. And I still feel the same wonderful feeling when I think about it. My mom loves me.

From those few flashbacks, I see that I had a mom who nurtured, disciplined, and loved me. But the greatest of these is love.

❤

Take time today to thank your mom for her unconditional love, and then thank the Lord, the greatest Lover of all, for His.

Firing Squad

"But Jesus went to the Mount of Olives. At dawn he appeared again in the temple courts, where all the people gathered around him, and he sat down to teach them. The teachers of the law and the Pharisees brought in a woman caught in adultery. They made her stand before the group and said to Jesus, 'Teacher, this woman was caught in the act of adultery. In the Law Moses commanded us to stone such women. Now what do you say?' They were using this question as a trap, in order to have a basis for accusing him.

"But Jesus bent down and started to write on the ground with his finger. When they kept on questioning him, he straightened up and said to them, 'If any one of you is without sin, let him be the first to throw a stone at her.' Again he stooped down and wrote on the ground.

"At this, those who heard began to go away one at a time, the older ones first, until only Jesus was left, with the woman still standing there. **Jesus straightened up and asked her, 'Woman, where are they? Has no one condemned you?'**

"'No one, sir,' she said.

" 'Then neither do I condemn you,' Jesus declared. 'Go now and leave your life of sin.' "

—John 8:1–11

One of the hardest things for me to overcome as a mom was what I had said about other people's children before I had any of my own. As a high school and college student I worked in retail, and I was often guilty of making quick judgments (actually misjudgments) about parents and their children (especially active, energetic children, such as those God gave me). Can you believe, with all the wisdom of a 19-year-old, single, childless woman, I once recommended the book *The Strong-Willed Child* to a couple struggling with a toddler in my store? Oh boy, have I ever had to repent for that one! All the foolish things I have thought or said have come back to me with the accuracy of a firing squad at my lowest, most desperate times as a parent.

Unfortunately, at times I'm still guilty of being critical of other moms, rather than supportive. Who knows why, but for some reason, we women, who are able to develop the most intimate relationships within a small circle of friends, seem to have a hard time supporting each other on the whole, as womankind. It's as though we're involved in some kind of weird competition where we earn points by detailing others' faults—so we dissect each other's choices and methods in order to validate our own.

John's fascinating account of Jesus' encounter with the adulteress reveals with great clarity the lowly existence of women in that ancient culture. This poor, lonely woman was surrounded by a pack of arrogant, obnoxious men, some of whom she must have known *personally*. Where were her friends? Did she have any? None of her own gender came to her aid with a support group or a legislative campaign or a media blitz on adulteresses' rights. No, it took the sinless Savior to remind her accusers that they had all fallen short of God's standard. Whether they were judging her out of their own ignorance, or in order to prove themselves, they were unable to "trap" (verse 6) the Lord Jesus, for He knew their motives. He knew their hearts, and He knew hers as well.

There are no perfect moms (and, by the way, no perfect children either, regardless of what your baby's grandparents say). However, if an adulteress can be acquitted by a carpenter's compassion, surely a good mom can become a better mom when she is commended rather than condemned. Let us not judge ourselves or others then, but commit today to supporting the mothers we know through prayer, a kind word, or a reassuring note. After all, your baby's mother-in-law is out there . . . somewhere.

❤

Ask God to show you a way to
encourage another mother today.

In the Trenches

"As the deer pants for streams of water,
  so my soul pants for you, O God.
My soul thirsts for God, for the living God.
  When can I go and meet with God?
My tears have been my food
  day and night,
while men say to me all day long,
  "Where is your God?"
These things I remember
  as I pour out my soul:
how I used to go with the multitude,
  leading the procession to the house of God,
with shouts of joy and thanksgiving
  among the festive throng.
Why are you downcast, O my soul?
  Why so disturbed within me?
Put your hope in God,
  for I will yet praise him,
  my Savior and my God."

—Psalm 42:1–6a

Sitcoms are fond of showing pregnant women in all sorts of comedic situations, and one part of pregnancy that is always good for a laugh is food cravings. From pickles and ice cream for breakfast to the mad dash for an anchovy pizza at 2:00 A.M., many women find television moms to be the only people they "know" who have had prenatal cravings. This was true of my friend Janie (name has been changed).

Janie was a registered nurse, and she had never put much stock in the idea of cravings. One morning toward the end of her second pregnancy, however, Janie wanted some chocolate milk. In fact, she *really* wanted some chocolate milk! She put it off, telling herself she really didn't want it. She spent the day going through her regular housework, playing with her 2-year-old, and trying not to think about a cold glass of rich, creamy chocolate milk. She began to believe that she was losing her mind! Though she did her best to control it, she had a full-blown craving for chocolate milk. Since she refused to respond to it, she was literally frantic by the end of the day.

When her husband arrived home, she managed to tell him she needed a few things at the store (she was afraid he would laugh at her) and raced to the closest market. Janie, at the time about seven or eight months pregnant, was quite a sight as she made a beeline for the dairy section and grabbed several cartons of chocolate milk. After making her purchase, Janie barely made it to her car before she downed a pint, satisfying her craving, tears streaming down her face from sheer relief!

Oh Christian sister! My prayer is that we will have a desire for Jesus that leaves us quite literally frantic until He satisfies it. Here we are in the trenches of motherhood! How in the world do we find time to make that connection we so desperately long for with Christ? Mary Farrar writes in her book, *Choices*:

"When the children are toddling about, your ability for 'quiet time' alone with the Lord is often completely out of your control, and many times is impossible. Unless you can rise each day at five for a rich, quiet time in Scripture, or unless you can stay alert for a deep, thoughtful time in the Word during afternoon nap time (I usually sacked out!), those are just plain tough years for spending quiet, quality time alone with the Lord.

"That doesn't change your need to be alone with God or to receive input from His Word. But there are all sorts of creative ways for you to gain the input you need at this stage of life (like listening to tapes while you are nursing, praying while you are cooking or driving, joining a mother's group, getting away for time with God on a Saturday when your husband is home). If you are not rising for a quiet time every morning, perhaps you really need the sleep! God understands your situation. He knows you're doing the best you can in this phase of life."

When you tell the Lord you are longing for Him,

He'll fulfill that yearning. He is faithful. Watch for those opportunities as He provides them. Expect to hear His voice when you turn on Christian radio. Count on your Sunday school teacher, small group leader, or pastor to have a special message for you when you attend services. When you grab a minute to pick up a devotional book, be ready to receive His Word in the selected Scripture. Isaiah 44:3 says, *"I will give you abundant water for your thirst and for your parched fields"* (TLB).

And what if you don't have that longing? Then just ask Him. He will see to it. He's your Father, and He will provide what you need. He is your satisfaction.

💜

What is your soul's desire? Tell it to Jesus.

Disorderly Conduct

"Once when they had finished eating and drinking in Shiloh, Hannah stood up. Now Eli the priest was sitting on a chair by the doorpost of the LORD's temple. **In bitterness of soul Hannah wept much and prayed to the LORD.** *And she made a vow, saying, 'O LORD Almighty, if you will only look upon your servant's misery and remember me, and not forget your servant but give her a son, then I will give him to the LORD for all the days of his life, and no razor will ever be used on his head.'*

"As she kept on praying to the LORD, Eli observed her mouth. Hannah was praying in her heart, and her lips were moving but her voice was not heard. Eli thought she was drunk and said to her, 'How long will you keep on getting drunk? Get rid of your wine.'

"'Not so, my lord,' Hannah replied, 'I am a woman who is deeply troubled. I have not been drinking wine or beer; I was pouring out my soul to the LORD. Do not take your servant for a wicked woman; I have been praying here out of my great anguish and grief.'"

"Eli answered, 'Go in peace, and may the God of Israel

grant you what you have asked of him.'

"She said, 'May your servant find favor in your eyes.' Then she went her way and ate something, and her face was no longer downcast.

"Early the next morning they arose and worshiped before the LORD and then went back to their home at Ramah. Elkanah lay with Hannah his wife, and the LORD remembered her. So in the course of time Hannah conceived and gave birth to a son. She named him Samuel, saying, 'Because I asked the LORD for him.'"

—I Samuel 1:9–20

When I was 17 years old, a friend of mine discovered she was pregnant. Luci (all the names in this story have been changed) had become promiscuous after her parents' divorce. She had several boyfriends. She wasn't sure which one was the father of her baby. She feared the response she might get from her parents if they learned of her situation, so she decided to get an abortion. At the time, I encouraged and supported her decision. I came to deeply regret doing that.

Just a couple of days after Luci and I discussed her situation, I was babysitting in the home of family friends. Their young son who ran about happily had been adopted just a couple of years before, and Jack and Lynda were on a waiting list for another child, a sibling for him. Because they could receive word of a child at any time, Lynda had the nursery ready and waiting. After I had put their little boy to bed I wandered in and looked around. It welcomed me with quiet anticipation. The crib covers were smooth. A motionless mobile was waiting to spin.

The diapers were stacked neatly on a changing table. On the wall hung the beautiful verse:

Not flesh of my flesh,
nor bone of my bone,
but yet, miraculously, my own!
Never forget for a single minute,
you weren't born under my heart,
but in it.

Waves of conviction washed over me. What a terrible mistake I had made! I ran to the telephone to call Luci. It was the wrong choice! Lots of people like Jack and Lynda would love a chance to raise her baby. I wish I could say that Luci chose to have her baby, but it wouldn't be true. She became angry with me for changing my mind and went ahead with her plans.

It is terribly difficult to understand why a teenager with multiple partners finds herself pregnant and a married, Christian woman finds herself infertile. There is no making sense of that one. Questioning the fairness of life only leads to resentment and hostility. That is what Hannah had been doing. When she brought her bitterness to the Lord, with honesty and vulnerability, she was able to leave it there. She went home then and waited, in quiet anticipation.

Hannah holds a place in God's Word and in every woman's heart because she trusted God in the midst of her trials and in spite of them. God blessed her with a child, and if you are reading this book, in His perfect timing, He has blessed you as well.

❤

Thank God today that, whatever your circumstance, you chose life.

Tour of Duty

"When the man Elkanah went up with all his family to offer the annual sacrifice to the LORD and to fulfill his vow, **Hannah did not go. She said to her husband, 'After the boy is weaned, I will take him and present him before the LORD, and he will live there always.'**

"'Do what seems best to you,' Elkanah her husband told her. 'Stay here until you have weaned him; only may the LORD make good his word.' So the woman stayed at home and nursed her son until she had weaned him.

"After he was weaned, she took the boy with her, young as he was, along with a three-year-old bull, an ephah of flour and a skin of wine, and brought him to the house of the LORD at Shiloh. When they had slaughtered the bull, they brought the boy to Eli, and she said to him, 'As surely as you live, my lord, I am the woman who stood here beside you praying to the LORD. I prayed for this child, and the LORD has granted me what I asked of him. So now I give him to the LORD. For his whole life he will be given over to the LORD.' And he worshiped the LORD there."

—1 Samuel 1:21–28

Have you ever promised to do something for someone, and when the time came, you really didn't want to go through with it? Taking that notion a step further, have you ever made a deal with God and then gone back on your word to Him? Or longed to?

Imagine Hannah, in the throes of her burdensome barrenness; she longs for a child and promises God that if He will just give her one, she will give him back! Many of us Christian mothers are big on talking about how we want to give our children back to God, but when we speak of that, we are talking in the spiritual realm, in the way of the intangible. Hannah knew what she was saying when she told God she would give her baby back to Him. She knew she was saying she would take her baby back to God's temple and leave him there. What she couldn't have understood, as a childless woman, was how much it would grieve her to do so. In fact, I'm sure it was the most difficult thing she would ever have to do. We skip over the emotions that were certainly there, though not recorded. Why should God document the obvious? Certainly a woman who felt such intense emotional heartbreak over her infertility would in no way be cold, hard, or detached when it came to leaving her baby at the temple.

Middle Eastern culture indicates that, most likely, Samuel was about three years of age, possibly four, when Hannah took him back to the temple and left him there with Eli. How did she explain to this little person what she was going to do that day? Had she been preparing him and herself all along? I stand amazed at her faithfulness to God. I wonder, could I have made good on a promise such as that? Could I have released my beloved son? Every step of the way to the temple, Hannah was faced with a choice. God was with her as she completed her tour of duty. Now He would take over.

Many people don't know that former President George Bush and his beloved wife Barbara had a daughter, Robin, who died at the age of three and a half from leukemia. They completed their tour of duty with this precious girl by spending many months in a New York City hospital. Of the hospital experience, Mrs. Bush writes in her memoir:

> "It was an extraordinary experience, and in a strange kind of way, we learned how lucky we were. We met people there who had only one child. We had three. We met people who did not love each other. We loved each other very much. . . . We had the most supportive family, and we shared. We had friends who helped us. Financially, we were very lucky, as our insurance covered almost everything.
>
> "And last, but not least, we believed in God. That has made an enormous difference in our lives, then and now."

In truth, none of us knows how long we have to raise our children. We aren't given an itinerary and a duty roster when we arrive at Fort Baby. We don't know how long we'll be asked to serve. But we can take comfort in knowing that we follow one who is the King of kings and the Lord of lords.

In her own strength, Hannah could have never deliberately left that little boy at the temple. Neither can we Christian mothers make good on our intention of dedicating our children completely to the Lord. We too often grab them back, thinking foolishly that they are better off in our arms than His. But Elkanah had it right when he said, *"may the LORD make good his word"* (verse 23). If it is your heart's desire to give your baby to the Lord, trust Him to keep you faithful throughout your tour of duty.

❤

**Ask God today for the courage to
dedicate your baby to Him.**

Rations

"Drink water from your own cistern,
 running water from your own well.
Should your springs overflow in the streets,
 your streams of water in the public squares?
Let them be yours alone,
 never to be shared with strangers.
May your fountain be blessed,
 and may you rejoice in the wife of your youth.
A loving doe, a graceful deer—
 may her breasts satisfy you always,
 may you ever be captivated by her love."
—Proverbs 5:15–19

During World War II, American troops were comprised not only of soldiers, but also of citizens back home. Everyone stateside was called upon to make their contribution to the war effort by doing without. For the most part, people were willing to do their share in a joint effort to gain victory. Their sacrifices of rationed food and gasoline seemed trivial when paralleled with the one that thousands of young men were willing to make with their very lives. People took home inventories and salvaged all kinds of scrap material, from worn-out tires and cooking grease to ladies' stockings. Yes, even sexy silk and nylon legwear took on a sensible role when it was recycled to produce items such as parachutes and gunpowder bags for the boys overseas.

If you are nursing your baby, it may occur to your husband that what were once the objects of his affection and passion are now being used very practically. And it may seem a bit odd to him that while your breasts are fuller and rounder than ever before, he can't even touch them without you fussing at him because they're sore, or you're exhausted, or he has set off that "let-down" reflex. (I was so thankful when an experienced mom told me that as long as I was nursing, I would need to wear a bra during sex! That piece of advice went a long way toward my comfort—if not my enjoyment—during that first year. By the way, if your milk comes down while you are reading this devotion, I apologize.)

During these first six weeks, your love life must be strictly rationed. Though sex does not have to be a casualty of war, it will be on inactive duty. I pray your husband will be the epitome of grace and understanding during this time. Most doctors recommend a hiatus from intercourse of four to six weeks. This is in your best interest, Mom—hormonally, physically, emotionally, and otherwise. When it is time to resume those relations, you may find that you are dealing with issues you have not experienced before, such as a lowered sex drive and vaginal dryness. Stormie Omartian, in her book *The Power of a Praying Wife*, offers some terrific advice for mothers of little ones:

"When your husband communicates to you what he has in mind, as only a husband can do, don't roll your eyes and sigh deeply. Instead, say, 'Okay, give me fifteen minutes.' (Or ten or twenty, or whatever you need.) During that time, do something to make yourself feel attractive. For example, take a shower or a relaxing bath. Put on scented body lotion or his favorite perfume. (Have perfume you wear only for these times alone with him.) Comb your hair. Wash your face and prepare it with products that make your skin look dewy and fresh. Put on lip gloss and blush. Slip into lingerie you know he finds irresistible. Don't worry about your imperfections; he's not thinking about them. If you feel self-conscious, wear a beautiful nightgown that covers areas that bother you. While you're doing this, pray for God to give you renewed energy, strength, vitality, and a good attitude. Hopefully, when you're ready, your husband will find you were worth the wait. You'll be surprised at how much better a sex partner you are when you feel good about yourself. He'll be happier and you'll both sleep better. This is a small investment of time to see great rewards in your marriage."

Remember that you and your husband made this baby. You were a couple, united by God, before He added this blessing of a family. You will go back to being a twosome when this child is grown and gone. In the years ahead, your marriage will go through times of passion and times of practicality. Even if you have to ration your body, don't restrain your love, but liberally express it with kindness and affection. As your husband respects your need for recovery, I pray that he is reminded that parenting is a team effort. His selflessness will go a long way in making sure you are comfortable and completely healed.

Use this time of abstinence to concentrate on your spiritual fulfillment in the Lord. Remember the ultimate sacrifice paid for you by your loving Bridegroom, Jesus Christ. His desire is for you to have a passionate faith, whether you are on the mountain, in the valley, or somewhere on the practical plateau of everyday living.

❤

Praise God today for the husband He gave you.

MIA: The American Mom

"Brothers, think of what you were when you were called. Not many of you were wise by human standards; not many were influential; not many were of noble birth. **But God chose the foolish things of the world to shame the wise; God chose the weak things of the world to shame the strong.** *He chose the lowly things of this world and the despised things—and the things that are not—to nullify the things that are, so that no one may boast before him. It is because of him that you are in Christ Jesus, who has become for us wisdom from God—that is, our righteousness, holiness and redemption. Therefore, as it is written: 'Let him who boasts boast in the Lord.'"*

—I Corinthians 1:26–31

The military term "KP" actually grew out of a slang phrase revealing soldiers' contempt for kitchen duty. It was such an unpleasant, grubby, obscure task that they began to mockingly call those who worked it "kitchen police." But if our soldiers had no sustenance, how long would they survive? If they ate their meals in unsanitary conditions, how long would they be fit to fight? It seems everywhere we turn, our culture has made a laughingstock of thankless yet crucial tasks—from sanitation workers to public school teachers. Yet we celebrate our sports superstars and Hollywood elite for the empty entertainment they provide, and we pay them richly for it. Is it any wonder that it's not popular to be a godly, Christian mom anymore?

During World War II, when Eleanor Roosevelt toured hospitals and Red Cross clubs in the Pacific, she was viewed by the troops as much more than simply the First Lady of the United States. As one soldier recalled, "She was something . . . none of us had seen in over a year, an American mother" (quoted in *Decade of Triumph: The 40s*, by Time-Life Books). Since those days, our country somehow moved from viewing mother as the lovely June Cleaver to the brash comedienne Roseanne. Whether art imitated life or vice versa, we have gone the wrong way, baby!

I believe that for each individual woman, the move is made from "active duty" to "missing in action" (MIA) when she chooses to put her own selfish desires ahead of what is best for her family. In our "me first" society, God's standard of servant motherhood is alien, outdated, and incompatible with the notion of today's mom, who can "have it all." You simply can't have it all. Somewhere along the way, sacrifices have to be made. Who will make them? You? Or your baby?

Dear Christian sister, this new job of yours—raising your child—is regarded as unimportant by the world. (If you don't believe that, take a look at the wages and benefits paid to childcare workers in this country. We don't put any money in it because we think anybody can do it.) Don't believe Satan's lies, not even for a second. It will not be the corporate world that will save America, not the media, not the politically correct, not the government, and certainly not Hollywood's idea of family values. It will not be the underpaid, overworked, exhausted women in daycare centers who are trying to handle 15 children at a time. It will be godly mothers, going about their daily duties for the least of these, praying at all times.

When God assigns you KP, I pray He won't find you MIA.

❤

Pray today that our society will again consider parenting an "active duty."

AWOL: My Paycheck!

*"These twelve Jesus sent out with the following instructions: 'Do not go among the Gentiles or enter any town of the Samaritans. Go rather to the **lost sheep** of Israel. As you go, preach this message: "The kingdom of heaven is near." Heal the sick, raise the dead, cleanse those who have leprosy, drive out demons. **Freely you have received, freely give.** Do not take along any gold or silver or copper in your belts; take no bag for the journey, or extra tunic, or sandals or a staff; for the **worker is worth his keep.**'"*
—Matthew 10:5–10

When Jesus sent out the disciples, He gave them several instructions: evangelize the world for Christ, give freely of our resources and our lives, and rely on our great and mighty God to meet our every need. We can certainly apply these same directives to our lives today, as Christians, knowing that whatever we do in life, we have been given the same mission as the apostles. Let today's passage speak directly to you as a new mother, and substitute "the lost sheep" with your baby's name; insert the name of your town in the place of "Israel." Now please take a moment to re-read the Scripture.

Oh, dear mother, what an impact you can make on this world if you hear Christ speaking to you of the importance of that babe in your arms. This is a life with eternal significance! You have a power like no other because you are that child's mother. You are the one who will influence your baby toward or away from Christ. He has given you a lost sheep. Will you take on the menial yet monumental tasks of a shepherd?

If you are making a change from the workaday world to the home, you will quickly discover that one absurdity about your new role as mother is that it lacks a paycheck! The most demanding, exhausting, stressful job in the world has no financial dividends, no 401k plan, no insurance benefits, and most unfortunately, no overtime pay. Yet the job description seemingly defies the capabilities of any one person.

Linda Weber defines the job of mothering. Are you ready for this? A mother is:

- **baby feeder**, changer, bather, rocker, burper, hugger
- **listener** to crying and fussing and thousands of questions
- **picker-upper** of food and debris cast on the floor
- **problem solver**, determiner of action, and the one who gives those talks to whomever needs them

- **phone messenger**, the reminder of responsibilities
- **comforter**, encourager, counselor
- **hygienist**
- **linguistic expert** for two-year-old dialects
- **trainer** of baby-sitters
- **listener**—for the husband as well as the children—about their day, their needs, their concerns, their aspirations
- **teacher** of everything from how to chew food to how to drive a car
- **assistant** on school projects
- **questioner**, prober to promote thinking
- **censor** of TV, movies, and books
- **reader** of thousands of children's books
- **planner** and hostess of children's birthday parties
- **planner** and hostess of adult dinner parties
- **short order cook** for those meals after the family's dinner that budding athletes depend upon
- **central control** for getting the appliance fixed or the carpet shampooed
- **executioner** of ants, roaches, wasps, and other pests
- **resident historian** in charge of photo albums, baby books, and school record books
- **resident encyclopedia** source for all those hard questions
- **officer** of the day, on call for any emergency
- **defroster** of the freezer
- **food preservation expert**
- **family secretary**, confirming dinner reservations, travel, and accommodations

- **corresponder** to the sick, the celebrating, or the generous
- **keeper** and locator of birth certificates and other valuable documents
- **ironer** of wrinkles
- **appointment desk** for the family's visits to the doctor, the dentist, the orthodontist, the barber, and the mechanic
- **seeker of God**
- **one who prays**
- **cleaner** of the oven, the drawers, the closets, the garage, the curtains, the bedding, the windows, and even the walls
- **refinisher** of furniture
- **emergency medical technician** and "ambulance" driver
- **hubby's romantic, attentive spouse**
- **enjoyer** of those moments when nothing is happening, no one is calling, nothing demands attention.

—From *Mom, You're Incredible!* by Linda Weber

Yes, soldier, your paycheck is AWOL: Absent Without Leave. Depend on God to supply your needs, and He will. He will even provide you with a paycheck—a different kind of paycheck. It happens when you least expect it, and it comes in various forms. Some of the best "paychecks" I have ever gotten have been the times my three children have said, "I love you" first. Or a sticky, wet kiss for no reason at all. Or a "Mommy, you look beautiful!" on a hectic Sunday morning. You may even get a paycheck from a stranger, who stops at your table in a crowded restaurant and compliments your children for being well behaved.

You see, God's idea of wealth is so much different from ours. He values the eternal. He reminds us to store up for ourselves *"treasures in heaven, where moth and rust do not destroy, and where thieves do not break in and steal"* (Matthew 6:20). Heaven's treasures will be the people we take with us. As you reconcile His way of remuneration, remember: you are worth your keep to Him, forever.

💜

Praise God for His provision and
for the "paychecks" to come!

Day 31

Sudden Impact

"Then Deborah said to Barak, 'Go! This is the day the Lord has given Sisera into your hands. Has not the Lord gone ahead of you?' So Barak went down Mount Tabor, followed by ten thousand men. At Barak's advance, the Lord routed Sisera and all his chariots and army by the sword, and Sisera abandoned his chariot and fled on foot. But Barak pursued the chariots and army as far as Harosheth Haggoyim. All the troops of Sisera fell by the sword; not a man was left.

"Sisera, however, fled on foot to the tent of Jael, the wife of Heber the Kenite, because there were friendly relations between Jabin king of Hazor and the clan of Heber the Kenite.

"Jael went out to meet Sisera and said to him, 'Come, my lord, come right in. Don't be afraid.' So he entered her tent, and she put a covering over him.

"'I'm thirsty,' he said. 'Please give me some water.' She opened a skin of milk, gave him a drink, and covered him up.

"'Stand in the doorway of the tent,' he told her. 'If someone comes by and asks you, "Is anyone here?" say "No."'

"But Jael, Heber's wife, picked up a tent peg and a hammer and went quietly to him while he lay fast asleep, exhausted. She drove the peg through his temple into the ground, and he died.

"Barak came by in pursuit of Sisera, and Jael went out to meet him. 'Come,' she said, 'I will show you the man you're looking for.' So he went in with her, and there lay Sisera with the tent peg through his temple—dead.

"On that day God subdued Jabin, the Canaanite king, before the Israelites. And the hand of the Israelites grew stronger and stronger against Jabin, the Canaanite king, until they destroyed him."

—Judges 4:14–24

Prayer often leads us to action. While we may spend much time on our knees talking to God and presenting our requests to Him, we also need to be listening to His voice, ready to heed His instructions to us. Today and tomorrow, we will look at an often-overlooked woman in the Bible, a woman who was prepared when God called her to active duty.

Today's Scripture finds Israel struggling under the oppression of Jabin, a king of Canaan. They cried out to the Lord for help. God heard Israel's prayers and sent His word through the prophetess Deborah. She told a man named Barak that God would give him victory over Sisera, the leader of Jabin's army. Barak was hesitant to accept this prophecy, with good reason. After all, Sisera's army was composed of 900 iron chariots, and Israel had been under his thumb for 20 years. He told Deborah that he was not going to war unless she went with him. Deborah agreed to go along, but she told Barak that *"because of the way you are going about this, the honor* [of the victory] *will not be yours, for the LORD will hand Sisera over to a woman"* (verse 9).

So Barak and an army of 10,000 men pursued Sisera and his army. By the power of Israel's God, they killed all of his troops, every single man—except Sisera himself, who abandoned his chariot and ran. He made it to the tent of Jael, the wife of Heber the Kenite. The Kenites were not Israelites, though they lived among them and accepted their God. These Kenite tribesmen were known for their plain, quiet, and even lonely way of living. At the time of this battle, the Kenites would actually have been considered a neutral society because there were *"friendly* [meaning without hostility] *relations between Jabin king of Hazor and the clan of Heber the Kenite"* (verse 17). As the events unfold, however, we see that Jael was anything but neutral with regard to this battle.

While Barak was summoned by Deborah with a word from God, Jael, as far as we know from Scripture, did not receive audible instructions from anyone. Instead, God met Jael where she was, at home, and gave her the opportunity to do something that would impact her whole country. She had no prophet to relay God's message, as did Barak. Unlike a modern-day Christian woman, she didn't have the Bible in multiple translations to guide her. She didn't have Christian radio or television to keep her posted on current events; yet within her isolated lifestyle, the world came to her doorstep. Because she was ready and willing, an untrained, uneducated housewife succeeded in capturing and killing the mighty Sisera—who had eluded the great warrior Barak and managed to escape the violent bloodshed that destroyed his entire army. How great is the glory of our God! He uses the *unlikely* to do the *unimaginable* with *unbeatable* results!

The world has come to your door, my sister. God wrapped it in a tiny, soft, sweet package, and He's given you the opportunity to make an impact. How?

- Introduce your child to Jesus Christ.
- Raise a child who knows the difference between right and wrong.
- Teach your child how to pray: for her home, her church, her government, and Christian missionaries.
- Model a Christian marriage of faith and forgiveness before your child.
- Tell your child you love her.
- Show her your love with your time.

Jael was willing to put aside the confusion and fear she must have been feeling and trust God. She didn't really know what she was doing, but she knew whose side she was on. She recognized the enemy. She realized the value of the moment, of singular opportunity. This was the chance of a lifetime. She didn't let it pass her by, and neither should you.

If staying at home appeals to you at all, don't sell it short. Like the Kenites, stay-at-home moms may be known as well for their plain, quiet, and often lonely way of living; yet they are seizing the days of childhood that can never be replaced. Days that, contrary to that stereotype, see plenty of action and adventure! Imagine what can be accomplished in a home where Christ is the head of the household. Are you prepared to invest in eternity? Are you ready to look at this time in your life from a God's-eye view? More on Jael tomorrow.

♥

Pray today that your child will impact the world for Christ.

At the Front Lines

"Most blessed of women be Jael,
  the wife of Heber the Kenite,
  most blessed of tent-dwelling women.
He asked for water, and she gave him milk;
  in a bowl fit for nobles she brought him curdled milk.
Her hand reached for the tent peg,
  her right hand for the workman's hammer.
She struck Sisera, she crushed his head,
  she shattered and pierced his temple.
At her feet he sank,
  he fell; there he lay.
At her feet he sank, he fell;
  where he sank, there he fell—dead."
                                        —Judges 5:24–27

Jael is simply going through her everyday tasks when Sisera approaches her tent. Wasn't Moses tending sheep when God spoke to him from a burning bush? The Heavenly Host appeared to a bunch of working-class shepherds during the night shift.

A Samaritan woman was going about her daily duties when she met the Savior at the town well. God speaks to us where we are: He is there in the ho-hum of life as mightily as He is in the supernatural, whiz-bang, glorified, once-in-a-great-while mountaintop experiences. Do you recognize Him in the routine? I believe Jael did.

Sisera has been in a battle, and he's been running as fast as his legs will carry him. We can imagine that when Jael saw him, she saw a frightened, sweaty, panting warrior who was still looking over his shoulder. She went out to meet him and ushered him into her tent, where she showered him with the customary hospitality one would give an honored guest. When he asked for water, she gave him fresh milk. She made him feel so safe and secure in her home that he immediately went to sleep in the warm bed she offered him.

Does she sound like a manipulative, cold-blooded killer to you?

When Jael awoke that morning, was she planning to capture Sisera and murder him?

Did she have any idea that her simple tent would be at the front lines of this battle?

She may have hoped she could help Israel by offering a place for Hebrew soldiers to rest and hide, but she hardly knew the commander of the enemy's army would come to her! However, when he did show up, she was ready with a sharp mind and a keen faith in God.

What did she have to use? Chariots and swords? No. She used what was readily available to her: hospitality, food, and blankets. When that cruel, oppressive man fell asleep, she used her only weapons: a hammer and a tent peg. The Kenites were a nomadic people, and many times Jael had pitched her own tent. She used the rudimentary tools of her day to defeat King Jabin's own blood-and-guts general. In spite of the enemy's chariots of iron and horse-backed army, Israel's victory belonged to the God who glories in our weakness, who chooses the *"foolish things of the world to shame the wise"* (1 Corinthians 1:27a).

Mary Farrar writes in her book, *Choices*:

"It took me a while to come to grips with the big picture. To see that God is not as impressed with us as we are. Yes, He is well aware of our desires and gifts (He put them there in the first place), but He is far more concerned with growing us up, stretching us, humbling us, accomplishing a deeper work within us. He can do it through illness, through failure, through disappointment. He can do it through unexpected hardship. And without question He does it through the process of sacrificial motherhood. God uses such times in our lives to accomplish His greater purposes, to prepare us for a work we simply cannot see from our ant-like per-spective."

Yesterday, we talked about Barak, a guy who thought he saw the big picture: Sisera's 900 iron chariots versus 10,000 Israelite men on foot. His view was from the human vantage point, our "ant-like perspective," not the Lord's. Jael saw a weary commander seeking refuge and realized not only her opportunity but also her duty. She caught a glimpse of something bigger than herself, and with that in mind, she gained victory. Victory for all of Israel! Victory, not because of her own strength, but because her power was in the Lord.

Do you see the Lord in your weakness? Can you identify with His suffering and pain more now than ever before? Do you have a deeper sense of His divine love, knowing now, firsthand, the great love a parent feels? God has a plan for you, mom. Use what you have, and look for Him where you are.

> ♥
> **Pray that in the details of today,**
> **God will give you a glimpse of the big picture.**

Armed Forces

"If you make the Most High your dwelling—
even the LORD, who is my refuge—
then no harm will befall you,
no disaster will come near your tent.
For he will command his angels concerning you
to guard you in all your ways;
they will lift you up in their hands,
so that you will not strike your foot against a stone.
You will tread upon the lion and the cobra;
you will trample the great lion and the serpent.
'Because he loves me,' says the LORD, 'I will rescue him;
I will protect him, for he acknowledges my name.'"
—Psalm 91:9–14

When her first baby was six weeks old, my friend Tammie started a new job. She was a single parent, and while she wished she could be at home with her son, she had to work. God was faithful to her as she secured childcare from a trusted family friend. She returned to the workforce under the best possible circumstances for a person in her situation. Yet one day, she commented to me, "I wish I was still pregnant."

"Why?" I asked, surprised.

"Because when Zachary was inside of me," she explained wistfully, "I was able to take better care of him. I was with him all the time, and I could protect him from everything."

Some of you reading this book are completing maternity leave and getting ready to go back to work. I pray that the arrangements you have made for childcare are the absolute best you can give your baby outside of yourself. I want to offer you a word of encouragement, whether you are worried about returning to work and leaving your baby with a day-care worker or a sitter, or if you're just trying to go back to church and you hesitate to leave him with a church nursery worker (or even a grand-mother): When you can't be there, you can trust the Lord, who is always with His children. His heavenly host of armed forces is ready to battle on our behalf. They have set up camp around believers, and they always introduce themselves with the words, "Fear not."

Fear is a dangerous emotion. If we're honest, we'll admit that most of us deal with it daily, in one form or another. Worry is just another name for it. Fear is the absence of trust. It's a thief, robbing us of our peace of mind.

Bible teacher Beth Moore says in her book, *To Live Is Christ*:

"I know what it's like to let fear deplete your energy. . . . I was so afraid I would lose my first child to crib death that I could hardly rest. Every few hours I jumped out of bed to see if she was breathing. Losing a child wasn't my only fear. From the time my mother officially became a senior adult, I often cried on the way home from her house because I feared something might happen to her before I saw her next.

"Had either tragedy happened, all my sleepless nights or buckets of tears would have helped me not one bit. God finally taught me to redirect my energies toward getting to know Him and love Him through His Word, so I can be equipped for anything."

I have always been a super-cautious driver, partly out of good sense and partly out of fear. The road is hazardous. The children and I pray a prayer of protection every time we buckle up, before we even leave the driveway. Whenever one of the kids gets in the car with someone else, I beg the Lord for their safety. Somehow, I have always felt that my children were safest in the car with their dad or me. Just a few months ago, however, while stopped at a red light, I felt the tremendous impact of an 18-wheeler as it crashed into the back of my van. My two older children were with me, sitting together on the back seat. Any other time, Danya would have been sitting in the front passenger seat, and David would have been sitting directly behind me. I'm still not sure how it happened that they were both on the back seat, but incredibly, our lives were spared.

Although the kids weren't where they were "supposed" to be, God protected them, and He did this in a way that I could have never accomplished in my humanness, for even though I was driving, we were in harm's way. Even though my foolish pride wants to say I'm in control, I'm not. Even though I'm extremely careful, I cannot protect my kids from the unknown, no matter how much I worry about it. While there are times now (and times to come, I'm sure) when I may wish I could cocoon them once more in my womb, at some point or other I have to realize that my children are better off in God's hands, and I have to give them to Him and leave them there.

♥

Trust God with the one He has entrusted to you.

Your Uniform

"For our struggle is not against flesh and blood, but against the rulers, against the authorities, against the powers of this dark world and against the spiritual forces of evil in the heavenly realms. **Therefore put on the full armor of God, so that when the day of evil comes, you may be able to stand your ground, and after you have done everything, to stand.** *Stand firm then, with the belt of truth buckled around your waist, with the breastplate of righteousness in place, and with your feet fitted with the readiness that comes from the gospel of peace. In addition to all this, take up the shield of faith, with which you can extinguish all the flaming arrows of the evil one. Take the helmet of salvation and the sword of the Spirit, which is the word of God. And pray in the Spirit on all occasions with all kinds of prayers and requests. With this in mind, be alert and always keep on praying for all the saints."*

—Ephesians 6:12–18

We spend a lot of time at the ballpark during the summer. I must admit, after a long, hot summer day with the children underfoot, there is something strangely soothing about seeing them caged behind a barbed-wire dugout!

Conveniently for us this year, Danya and David are able to play together on the same team in the 5- to 8-year-old league. In this league, there are all kinds of degrees of experience among the children. Some of the kids at five years of age have been playing ball since they were toddlers. For some 8-year-olds, it is their first season. Of course, you can't always tell the experienced kids from the rookies until you see them play. I've seen coaches send the outfield back a few steps for an older kid who, it turns out, can't hit the ball. Likewise, I've seen coaches underestimate a squirt who can!

At one of our first games this season, a tall blonde girl came up to the plate. She was in a sparkling white uniform, ponytail tucked smoothly under her cap, and a batting glove on her right hand. She bounced right up to the plate with confidence, drew a line next to the base with her bat, and squared up. Obviously, this kid could play ball.

Strike 1!

Strike 2!

Strike 3!

Strikes 4–11! (In our league, you get to swing until you get a hit.)

The fans were stunned. This child looked like a ballplayer. She acted like a ballplayer. But she couldn't hit the ball. It was her first season; she didn't know how. She hadn't received any training, and she had no experience.

It's too bad that clothes *don't* make the man (or

141

woman). Wouldn't it be fun to put on a St. Louis Cardinals uniform and play baseball like Mark McGwire? Or, when your baby's sick, to be able to string a stethoscope around your neck and instantly make a diagnosis? What if you could don a black robe, grab a gavel, and acquire at once the wisdom and discernment of a Supreme Court judge? Most recruits receive a pair of boots and several sets of fatigues during the first week of boot camp. But does that make them soldiers? Of course not. Like my son David's Superman costume, it's fun to wear, but you still can't fly! Without the training and the hard work, the uniform doesn't really fit.

What do you dress in to be a mom? Perhaps you've traded in a "power suit" or some other career uniform for sweat pants and a t-shirt. (There will be days when you find yourself still in your nightclothes at noon!) More importantly, what do you wear to be a Christian? Today's Scripture has the answer. The Bible provides a full wardrobe for the Christian woman, no matter what line of work she's in. You may wear it everyday, and it's always in style with the Master Designer! You don't have to worry about washing this outfit—spit up and other baby bodily fluids won't do any damage. Leaky breasts won't rust this armor, nor will tears. And the belt of truth (thank God!) is one-size-fits-all!

Perhaps as a new mom you feel like that little ballplayer: you've got all the right equipment, and you're wearing the right clothes, and yet you feel as though every day you are striking out. Keep on swinging! God doesn't keep a record of our strikes. Like that little girl's dad, your Father just keeps cheering you on.

These first six weeks are an intense period of training. You will come out on the other side wearing a "mom" uniform that really fits. You'll grow into it! Mothering is part instinct, I readily admit; however, it is mostly day-by-day experience. It is learning by doing, by listening, by watching, and by praying. Think of the twelve disciples. When Jesus called them, He could have given them instantaneous, touch-the-hem-of-My-garment, complete knowledge of God. Instead, He took them through three years of daily training. Imagine the apostles' boot camp: living with Jesus Christ and learning by doing, by listening, by watching, and by praying. Even then, there was one among them who looked like a disciple, and sadly, was not.

❤

**As God teaches you today,
remember it's not the uniform, it's the training.**

Ceasefire

"Sing to the LORD, you saints of his;
    praise his holy name.
For his anger lasts only a moment,
    but his favor lasts a lifetime;
weeping may remain for a night,
    but rejoicing comes in the morning.

"When I felt secure, I said,
    'I will never be shaken.'
O LORD, when you favored me,
    you made my mountain stand firm;
but when you hid your face,
    I was dismayed.

"To you, O LORD, I called;
    to the Lord I cried for mercy:
'What gain is there in my destruction,
    in my going down into the pit?
Will the dust praise you?
    Will it proclaim your faithfulness?
Hear, O LORD, and be merciful to me;
    O LORD, be my help.'"

—Psalm 30:4–10

Part of your initiation into motherhood is the inevitable night shift. Some nights, Danya was just *awake*. She was just learning that nights were for sleeping. So we sat together in the rocking chair, her big baby eyes staring at me in a dark room. It was a sweet time. I had never seen a little face as beautiful as hers.

Some nights, however, I was relegated to walking my post, like a soldier, with a screaming baby rather than a rifle on my shoulder. I did everything to quiet her when she had bad nights. I tried running the vacuum, the bathroom fan, a humidifier, and watching the 3:00 A.M. reruns of *The Dick Van Dyke Show* on Nickelodeon. (She was not amused.)

I will never forget the first full night's sleep I got after Danya was born. I had worn my running shoes to bed, telling Rich, "There is no point in taking my shoes off. I'll be walking the floor in just a couple of hours." With that, I laid my head down on my pillow, with my feet hanging over the side of the bed. The next thing I knew it was morning! Rich's alarm clock woke me. This is exactly what went through my mind: *What time is it? That's Rich's alarm. We slept through the night! Oh no! There's something wrong with the baby!* Flying to her room, I found that Danya, as well, was just beginning to rouse from her first full night of sleep. Finally, a ceasefire. We were on our way to normal.

Do you long for a ceasefire from the demands of this new life? Do you wake up feeling as though you are at the beginning of a daily obstacle course, with nursing, diapering, and a ton of other chores looming before you like great tunnels, tires, and tightropes? This is not the life you're used to, is it? You don't feel like yourself, and you certainly don't look like yourself. You don't even smell like yourself! Who knew that this little bit of a person could rock your world with such great force?

It is exhausting meeting the demands of a baby 24 hours a day. Jesus found it quite tiring meeting the demands of throngs of people who clamored for healing and longed for His teaching. Even developing intimate bonds with his band of disciples took time and emotional energy. He needed to rest. He needed to get away.

In our culture, at best, that's what a vacation is for.

Weekly, that's what a Sabbath is for.

Daily, that's what naptime and a telephone answering machine are for.

And moment by moment, that is what your relationship with the Almighty God is for. As He stretches you to fit His idea of motherhood, remember: He is your help. Rely on Him every minute of the day and night. One morning soon, you'll wake up with your shoes on!

❤

Praise God for the night shift—I understand it comes back around when they are teenagers!

Peace Talks

"We all stumble in many ways. If anyone is never at fault in what he says, he is a perfect man, able to keep his whole body in check.

"When we put bits into the mouths of horses to make them obey us, we can turn the whole animal. Or take ships as an example. Although they are so large and are driven by strong winds, they are steered by a very small rudder wherever the pilot wants to go. **Likewise the tongue is a small part of the body, but it makes great boasts. Consider what a great forest is set on fire by a small spark.** *The tongue also is a fire, a world of evil among the parts of the body. It corrupts the whole person, sets the whole course of his life on fire, and is itself set on fire by hell.*

"All kinds of animals, birds, reptiles and creatures of the sea are being tamed and have been tamed by man, but no man can tame the tongue. It is a restless evil, full of deadly poison."
—James 3:2–8

During World War II, our nation was deeply concerned about the danger of Nazi spies. Enemy agents were real, and their mission was to sabotage

United States business and industry. The American people pulled together and were vigilant in guarding their country. They took extreme precautions, such as not issuing weather forecasts for two years, so as not to aid the enemy's bombing raids. Because the spies that had been caught could have easily passed for "Regular Joes," people were mindful that they could truly threaten the nation's security by simply saying the wrong thing to the wrong person. "Loose lips sink ships" became a popular slogan Americans used to remind each other of the risks we faced collectively. It's a phrase we still use today to illustrate the potentially damaging strength of our words.

Words do have power. God spoke our day into existence when He commanded, *"Let there be light"* (Genesis 1:3). Jesus spoke our eternity into being when He uttered, *"It is finished"* (John 19:30). We are made in God's image, and He has given us authority through our own words. We are able to kill and destroy with our words. On the other hand, our words enable us to speak life and healing, as well.

Several years ago, Danya was in a Mother's Day Out program once a week. There was one mom who dropped her son off every time with this kind of angry garbage pouring from her mouth: "Go on in there! I am so glad to be rid of him today. I thought I wouldn't stand it until I got here. We've had some kind of morning. But I am free today! I'm outta here."

It broke my heart—for both of them. No one wants to see a little kid being humiliated by his mother. And when I thought of all she was losing by selfishly giving in to a verbal tirade, I hurt for her, too. You see, I believe that every day we are living in a war zone, fighting Satan for our children and our families. Of course, Jesus Christ has won the war, but every day there are battles to be faced. Many of them can be won or lost with the weapon of our words.

You may have been given this advice as a newlywed: *"Do not let the sun go down while you are still angry"* (Ephesians 4:26). Let it apply to all of family life. At bedtime around here, each child is prayed for and talked with individually. If anything is bothering anyone, it comes out then (if it hasn't already). It is part of a nighttime routine that has evolved from rocking and singing to reading and talking and praying. These "peace talks" go a long way in a good night's rest for all of us. It helps us in building a foundation with our children of open communication, which is important now and will continue to be in the future. Satan is a wicked spy with a multitude of disguises who longs to sneak in and sabotage our Christian homes. We must be vigilant in guarding our families from morning to night, seeking to embrace, protect, and love them with our words.

♥

**Ask God for wisdom and discernment
in your choice of words today.**

Dog Tags

"With the tongue we praise our Lord and Father, and with it we curse men, who have been made in God's likeness. **Out of the same mouth come praise and cursing. My brothers, this should not be.** Can both fresh water and salt water flow from the same spring? My brothers, can a fig tree bear olives, or a grapevine bear figs? Neither can a salt spring produce fresh water."

—James 3:9–12

E ver thought about the cute little "dog tags" worn by soldiers? These are actually military identification tags that must be worn at all times by armed services personnel. They contain limited but essential information about the person wearing them: name, Social Security number, and blood type. They don't, however, provide any facts about the personality of the wearer, such as: great dancer, artist, generous giver, or loves to read.

Unfortunately, we tend to classify people in much the same way. Rather than attempting to explore someone's character, we opt to categorize. Without taking the time to get to know a personality, we label a person. (Remember high school?) We are all guilty of judging by appearance. In fact, Camille Lavington has written a book entitled, *You've Only Got Three Seconds*, in which she claims that "irreversible judgments" are formed within the first three seconds of meeting someone. I remember being taught that "you only have one chance to make a first impression," but if Camille Lavington is right, the pressure is on! Only three seconds!

Like it or not, the truth is that first impressions are not always accurate. Rich and I, and several other couples I know, wouldn't even be together if we had established an unwavering conviction on that first impression. It's important to get to know people from the inside out rather than from the outside in.

This applies to children, too. How many children have been falsely labeled in the preschool years? Or even as babies? Babies cry. Many times babies are hard to get along with. There are days when they are stubborn. There are days when they are cranky and hot-tempered. But please, don't label a child on the negative aspects of his personality, and don't allow anyone else to, either. Anne Ortlund has written an award-winning book called *Children Are Wet Cement*, in which she explains that we have a great deal of leeway in the development of our child's personality merely by the traits that we choose to affirm. This philosophy is straight from the Book of Proverbs. In Proverbs 12, the Bible tells us that with our godly speech we have the power to:

- **rescue** *"the speech of the upright rescues them"* (verse 6b)
- **prosper** *"from the fruit of his lips a man is filled with good things"* (verse 14a)
- **heal** *"the tongue of the wise brings healing"* (verse 18b)
- **cheer** *"a kind word cheers"* (verse 25b)

The opposite is true as well. The New Testament Book of James tells us, *"The tongue also is a fire, a world of evil among the parts of the body. It corrupts the whole person, sets the whole course of his life on fire, and is itself set on fire by hell"* (James 3:6). Ouch!

When David was about 10 months old, we were at Wal-Mart, and he was sitting in the shopping cart. He wore a mischievous smile on his face as one of the clerks started playing with him. She said to him, "Oh! You're a little devil, aren't you! Momma's got her hands full with you!"

I turned to this woman as calmly as I could and replied, "David is a sweet boy. He is a good boy. I'm thankful he's my son." As I quickly wheeled my cart away, I whispered a stern rebuke and rejected the words she had leveled at my child. I'm serious! Don't call my child names.

Did you ever see the *I Love Lucy* episode in which Lucy and Ethel steal John Wayne's concrete block from Grauman's Chinese Theatre? Ricky makes them take it back, but it gets broken, of course, before they can return it. They have to get John Wayne to do another one, and great comedy follows from Lucille Ball and quick-drying cement! They try to get clean prints of his boots and his signature again and again, and either the wet cement is marred before it dries, or the dried cement is broken before it is replaced. Hysterical!

I'm sure I was just as funny rebuking that salesclerk from behind a rack of clothes in Wal-Mart. In truth, her comment was quickly brushed away, and David's cement bears no lasting effects. However, "word power" works both ways. We can be a "fountain of life" (Proverbs 10:11), or we can foolishly spread slander and damage with our talk.

God, please help us as parents to affirm and encourage with our speech, to truly bless our children with our words. May we label the positive and lovingly discipline the negative in our kids, taking the time to love both the person and the personality.

❤

Thank God today for the affirming labels of *Christian*, *Wife*, and *New Mom*.

Mail Call

"Rejoice in the Lord always. I will say it again: Rejoice! Let your gentleness be evident to all. The Lord is near. Do not be anxious about anything, but in everything, by prayer and petition, with thanksgiving, present your requests to God. And the peace of God, which transcends all understanding, will guard your hearts and your minds in Christ Jesus.

"Finally, brothers, whatever is true, whatever is noble, whatever is right, whatever is pure, whatever is lovely, whatever is admirable—if anything is excellent or praiseworthy—think about such things. **Whatever you have learned or received or heard from me, or seen in me—put it into practice.** *And the God of peace will be with you."*

—Philippians 4:4–9

Don't you just love to get mail? Today's computer technology has allowed me to correspond with people from whom I never would have received an actual letter! It's a thrill, whether on paper or via electronic transit, to receive caring words from someone you love.

My mother kept a small baby book for me in which she wrote a few short letters, all before I turned three years old. It has been special to me ever since I learned how to read. Her love comes bursting through each word to tell me that I am very special.

I began keeping journals for my children with that precedent in mind. My plan is to give each child a completed journal as they approach adolescence, somewhere between the ages of 11 and 13. I have written in these little books the stories of their births, each one's special place in our family, and even some heartfelt advice on awkward adolescent issues that may be hard to discuss. Christmases and birthday celebrations are recorded, and in recent years I have had the great joy of writing down my children's salvation stories to protect those precious memories of their early decisions for Christ. I envision giving these journals to each child with some emotion and celebration, almost as a rite of passage—for them and for me. My goal is to convey through these books my love for them and each child's specialness.

Thank God for those inspiring letters from the apostle Paul in the New Testament. How would the early church (and the church today) have survived without those stirring letters written by a man whose life was completely transformed by the resurrected Christ? Through his advice, doctrinal teaching, and personal honesty, Paul gave the church something they would desperately need in order to survive and thrive: encouragement. When I think of what my children will need as teenagers, these journals become my battle plan of encouragement to get them through those growing up years so that they, too, will survive and thrive.

Here are some excerpts from my kids' journals:

Dear Danya:
Last Sunday was Mother's Day, and we had the parent-baby dedication service at Carmel. You were a doll through the whole thing, mesmerized by the church and the singer. We dedicated ourselves to raise you in the Word, teach you about Jesus, and pray for you always. We do pray that you will let Jesus be the Lord of your life and that you'll accept His salvation. He loves you so much, Danya, and He has a marvelous plan for your life. Listen to Him—be His girl first.

I love watching you grow.

Dear David:
You are the most precious, wonderful baby. You're so sweet, with a ready smile and a playful giggle. I love holding you, kissing you, and snuggling you. These moments are for such a short time. . . . We stopped in Greenbriar before heading home to Paducah, and Nana was telling you to "be a doctor, and add something to this world!" She was half-teasing, of course, but here's what I have to say: Do what makes you happy, because happy, Spirit-filled people are the ones who truly add the most to this world. Love Jesus, and spend your life (no matter what occupation you choose) connecting

others to Him.

Dear Derek:
How I love you, Little Bit! (That's what we call you!) David is crazy about you. He sometimes gets a little rough in his play, but you scarcely complain. And Sissy delights in being a little momma to you. You go to her bedroom door every morning to see if she's awake. . . . You're about to walk, young man; it won't be long before you do! My prayer is that you will walk in His steps, the steps of our master, Jesus Christ. His hand is on your life, Derek; He has a plan and a purpose for you. What will it be? He will show you.

I wrote in Danya's journal every month. Consequently, it was full even before David was born. The boys' books are not complete, but if something happened to me tomorrow (God forbid), they would have written evidence of my love. Moms think about those things, you know.

God did, too. He wrote down the story of His love for us. Whenever we need to feel His love, or be reminded of our specialness, all we need to do is read the Book He gave us. His love comes bursting through each word!

❤

**Thank God today for the sweet love letters
He's written to you.**

Day 39

M*A*S*H

"*Righteousness and justice are the foundation of your throne;*
love and faithfulness go before you.
Blessed are those who have learned to acclaim you,
who walk in the light of your presence, O LORD.
They rejoice in your name all day long;
they exult in your righteousness.
For you are their glory and strength,
and by your favor you exalt our horn.
Indeed, our shield belongs to the LORD,
our king to the Holy One of Israel."

—*Psalm 89:14–18*

Several years ago, I heard a sermon by Andy Stanley that changed my life. He pointed out that when we Christians watch television indiscriminately, we are allowing ourselves to be entertained by the very sin for which our Christ suffered and died. We're laughing and yukking it up in response to the sin that God responded to with the sacrifice of His only begotten Son. Since then, I am more particular about my choices for entertainment.

This makes it very difficult to find something to watch on TV! Sometimes, however, Rich and I will watch a M*A*S*H rerun after the kids go to bed. I'm not crazy about some of the shows, but as the character Father Mulcahy is developed an interesting thing happens. The presence of God is acknowledged. That makes this comedy/drama quite different from many television programs where there is no reference to God other than the misuse of His holy name to express shock, disgust, surprise, horror, etc. In their realistic depiction of the people who served our country so faithfully in the Korean war, the writers of M*A*S*H chose to include a Catholic chaplain who is authentic, not a stereotyped mockery of a man of the cloth but a real person who struggled along with everyone else to make sense out of the war. He is sincere, vulnerable, and genuine, respected by the others and recognized by them as having a relationship with the Almighty God.

When Father Mulcahy is part of a scene, it naturally takes on a different tone. It's his presence—the mere fact that he's there. This reminds me of the difference that can occur in our lives when we acknowledge the presence of God. Although we cannot see Him with our physical eyes, we can practice being aware of His very real closeness, as He inhabits our Christian walk. With every new morning, we have the opportunity of continual fellowship with Him, moment by moment. Could it be that it hinges solely on the awareness of His nearness? That sounds so simple, yet it's anything but easy. How do we obtain this consciousness of God and woman, dwelling together? My favorite Christian author, Anne Ortlund, tells us how in her book, *Fix Your Eyes on Jesus*:

> **"First, ask Him.** I know what I do when left to myself: I'm 'prone to wander—Lord, I feel it!—prone to leave the God I love.' Ask Him. He loves you to.
>
> **"Second, cooperate with Him.** Vote against your natural waywardness! Keep prompting yourself, to form the habit."

Now that you have a newborn around, aren't you conscious of him? Sure you are! There are pieces of him everywhere you look. "Diapers & wipes" are on the grocery list. Bottles are in the fridge. Crib sheets tumble in the dryer. A pacifier lies out of reach behind the couch. And you hear him. You smell him. You see him. You touch him. You kiss him.

You've been aware of him, however, since you found out that he existed, deep inside of you. Maybe in the beginning stages of your pregnancy, when doctor's visits were few and far between and you weren't yet "showing," your daily activities weren't quite as affected by your child. However, once you knew you were pregnant, you couldn't forget about it. As your belly began to swell with his life, it became evident to all that you were a mother. As weeks and then months ticked by, all you could think about was your baby. Everything you did, great or small, was influenced by his presence. And you couldn't even see him.

I wonder if we would be better Christians if when Christ entered our hearts, there was an obvious physical change, as with pregnancy—a no denying it, no covering it up, obvious to strangers, plain-as-the-nose-on-your-face kind of change. But as Anne Ortlund explains, the habit of practicing His presence "doesn't just 'happen.' **It begins with desire, and it continues with discipline.** It's not just automatic, it's learned—like somebody's being initiated into a fraternity or sorority, until they're at last in the fellowship."

I long to be in His fellowship, 24 hours a day. You may remember that the character of Father Mulcahy had no boundaries on M*A*S*H. In the eleven years that M*A*S*H was on television, he was in every type of setting, from the operating room to the officer's club. God is limitless, as well. Whether you acknowledge Him or not, He's there in the mess tent just as He's there in post-op. Let's start today, not only living *for* Him, but living *with* Him.

❤

**Pray today for God to work in you
the habit of practicing His presence.**

Shipping Out

"On the third day a wedding took place at Cana in Galilee. Jesus' mother was there, and Jesus and his disciples had also been invited to the wedding. **When the wine was gone, Jesus' mother said to him, 'They have no more wine.'**

"'**Dear woman, why do you involve me?' Jesus replied. 'My time has not yet come.'**

"**His mother said to the servants, 'Do whatever he tells you.'**

"Nearby stood six stone water jars, the kind used by the Jews for ceremonial washing, each holding from twenty to thirty gallons.

"Jesus said to the servants, 'Fill the jars with water'; so they filled them to the brim.

"Then he told them, 'Now draw some out and take it to the master of the banquet.'

"They did so, and the master of the banquet tasted the water that had been turned into wine. He did not realize where it had come from, though the servants who had drawn the water knew. Then he called the bridegroom aside and said, 'Everyone brings out the choice wine first and then the *cheaper wine after the guests have had too much to drink; but you have saved the best till now.'"*

—John 2:1–11

Jesus Christ had a mother. She is present, of course, at the beginning of His earthly life, and she is there at the foot of the cross when He gives it up. Also, His mother Mary is by His side, involved with Him, at the scene of His first recorded miracle: the wedding in Cana, where Jesus turns the water into wine. This passage is rich with meaning, but for the purposes of this little book, let's focus on the relationship between Christ and His mom.

Imagine the scene: a glorious festival of marriage, a truly lavish event. Mary is there with her son—her perfect, holy, righteous son. Did she ever entertain the idea that He would give her grandchildren? Is she perhaps wondering if Jesus might meet someone that He likes here at the wedding? Did she ever have her eye on a young Jewish maiden who might make Him a good wife?

The angel told her that this babe who was conceived within her by the Spirit of the Almighty God would be *"called the Son of the Most High."* He told her that *"The Lord God will give him the throne of his father David, and he will reign over the house of Jacob forever; his kingdom will never end"* (Luke 1:32b–33). Gabriel didn't mention anything about trumped-up charges, or a cross, or a murder, or a borrowed grave. Jesus is 30 years old now. Mary knows He's special! But I don't think she knows His immediate, inevitable future. (God must have spared her that, or she would have gone mad.)

Perhaps Mary notices confusion and murmuring among the servants and quickly realizes there is no more wine. *What a terrible humiliation for the host!* she thinks. One of the servants casts a glance her way. His fearful eyes confirm her suspicions. Mary knows these servants will be blamed and harshly punished for this error. The host, of course, will be the talk of the town for years to come for throwing a party and running out of wine. He will be laughed at by friend and foe alike. At this point, it wouldn't really matter whose fault it was, anyway. This is a problem with seemingly no way out. Mary genuinely hurts for all involved. Taking pains to be discreet, she quietly tells Jesus, "They've run out of wine."

Now here's Jesus—the ultimate guest. He's a storyteller, a joyful conversationalist who loves being around people. He replies casually, between bites, "Dear woman, what do you want me to do about it?" I imagine my Jesus, Mary's son, with a smile on His face. He is a doting son who knows full well what she wants Him to do. They have a special kind of connection; after all, He is *her* beloved Son, too. When He looks up from His plate into her eyes, she can see that He understands her concern for her friend's reputation and her compassion for the servants who will take the brunt of the blame, and she knows He cares about even this. He suddenly grows serious, as for a moment His manner changes. He knows she will not understand, but He says it anyway, *"My time has not yet come"* (verse 4b).

Something happens between this last comment

of Christ's, and Mary's telling the servants to *"Do whatever he tells you"* (verse 5b). I would like to suggest that Jesus and His mom are face to face during this encounter. They are eye to eye, heart to heart. That special chemistry between mother and son is a factor that must not be overlooked when looking over these verses. He is telling her that His time to die, His cross, has not yet come, but He's shipping out. This miracle that she thinks she is initiating is, in fact, the beginning of the end of His human life. He has shared so much with His mother. Yet, while He finds it hard to tell her what is going to happen, a part of Him wants her to know. But she's not there yet—she's not ready to hear it. She knows that He can do something about today's situation right now, and that is all she wants.

So what happened between the lines of verses four and five?

Did He smile?

Did He nod?

Did He shake His head laughingly at the transparency of His mother?

I don't know, but He acquiesced. He honored His mother. And with His consent, she directed the servants.

❤

Pray that God would bless a relationship between you and your child in which there is honor and respect on both sides, along with a Christ-like humility and love.

All in the Line of Duty

"On the third day a wedding took place at Cana in Galilee. Jesus' mother was there, and Jesus and his disciples had also been invited to the wedding. When the wine was gone, Jesus' mother said to him, 'They have no more wine.'

"'Dear woman, why do you involve me?' Jesus replied. 'My time has not yet come.'

"His mother said to the servants, 'Do whatever he tells you.'

"Nearby stood six stone water jars, the kind used by the Jews for ceremonial washing, each holding from twenty to thirty gallons.

"Jesus said to the servants, 'Fill the jars with water'; so they filled them to the brim.

"Then he told them, 'Now draw some out and take it to the master of the banquet.'

"They did so, **and the master of the banquet tasted the water that had been turned into wine. He did not realize where it had come from, though the servants who had drawn the water knew.** Then he called the bridegroom aside and said, 'Everyone brings out the *choice wine first and then the cheaper wine after the guests have had too much to drink; but you have saved the best till now.'"*

—John 2:1–11

I hope you recognized the Scripture above. We're looking at it again today, and for a third and final time tomorrow.

Pastor Jim Cymbala of the Brooklyn Tabernacle says in his book *Fresh Wind, Fresh Fire* that it is God's nature to be attracted to our weakness. Therefore, it is quite characteristic of God's Son, Jesus, to be present at the social event of the season, among scads of prominent people, and yet have His focus on the servants—servants who wouldn't even dream of being invited to this kind of high-society function. These people, whom the world defines as nameless, nothing, nobodies, are the ones chosen by God to be the first to see the glory of the Lord. Isn't that just like Him?

Let's understand the hopelessness of their situation. A Jewish wedding feast could go on for up to a week. During that time, it was the responsibility of the host, the master, to furnish food and drink. It was a terrible mark on the name of a family who failed to be properly prepared for this once-in-a-lifetime occasion. The singular fact that the servants were willing to listen to Jesus (to them He was an unknown guest) indicates the depth of their despair. They had nowhere to turn, so they were willing to do anything. They were willing to depend on Jesus instead of themselves. Who would have guessed that in this most desperate of situations these servants would meet the real Master?

God purposely equates the role of mother with servant. When Mary is told that she will become a mother, she calls herself a *"servant girl of the Lord"* (Luke 1:38, ERV). It is by God's design that humans are born fully dependent on another for survival. A mother is a servant to a totally helpless soul; that's God's perfect plan. In this we are reminded of His Son, who *"made himself nothing, taking the very nature of a servant,"* (Philippians 2:7) in order to save our helpless souls.

You are the primary caregiver and the sole sustenance for your baby at this time. This is a revelation for you and for your child. In the same way, God reveals His glory to us when we are "born again" into a life with Christ. Like an infant, we must come to a point of total dependence on the Lord, looking to Him as our primary caregiver and our sole sustenance.

Think of how quickly you respond to your baby's cries. Are you prompt to change those dirty diapers and bed sheets? Are you ready with breast or bottle when it's feeding time? That's all in the line of duty for a new mom. Embrace your role as servant! God is breathing His life into you, sister, forming in you the mind of Christ. You are truly serving God with every hug, every wipe, every pat on the back. Rely on Him. Trust Him when you feel overwhelmed by circumstances. You, too, will see the water turn to wine—and you will be the first to know where it came from.

❤

**Thank God for the work He began
and is completing in you.**

Graduation

"On the third day a wedding took place at Cana in Galilee. Jesus' mother was there, and Jesus and his disciples had also been invited to the wedding. When the wine was gone, Jesus' mother said to him, 'They have no more wine.'

"'Dear woman, why do you involve me?' Jesus replied. 'My time has not yet come.'

"His mother said to the servants, 'Do whatever he tells you.'

"Nearby stood six stone water jars, the kind used by the Jews for ceremonial washing, each holding from twenty to thirty gallons.

"Jesus said to the servants, 'Fill the jars with water'; so they filled them to the brim.

"Then he told them, 'Now draw some out and take it to the master of the banquet.'

"They did so, and the master of the banquet tasted the water that had been turned into wine. He did not realize where it had come from, though the servants who had drawn the water knew. Then he called the bridegroom aside and said, **'Everyone brings out the choice wine first and**

then the cheaper wine after the guests have had too
much to drink; but you have saved the best till now.'"
—John 2:1–11

Congratulations! You've made it through Baby Boot Camp! What a great feeling.

Have you seen some changes in yourself, mom? These first six weeks have opened your eyes to servanthood—to love that you never knew was in you to give. Think back and remember the first moment you saw your baby. Grab hold of that wonder, that bliss, that heart-stopping happiness that occurred upon your eyes' first taste of him or her! That, dear sister, is love at first sight. There is nothing like that first moment. Now it is a memory to treasure and savor for the rest of your life.

Isn't it amazing the changes you've seen in your baby? Life with your child will continue to get better and better. It doesn't go downhill. It is always evolving. Each day that baby is growing toward God's plan for his life, just as you are. You are part of each other's plan! You are each essential to the other's *becoming.*

God's plan is for you to train that child in the way he should go. You are not keeping him. You are preparing him. Solomon said that children are *"like arrows in the hands of a warrior"* (Psalm 127:4). Let us sharpen our arrows with prayer and the teaching of God's Word, so that we may send them out to pierce the darkness with the light of Jesus Christ. Then when our children leave home we will lose nothing but gain everything.

In our own ever-evolving relationship with the

Lord Jesus Christ, He reveals Himself to us continuously, when we ask. And indeed, He does save the best for last, when at last we shall see Him, *"face to face"* (1 Corinthians 13:12). Just as our children, however, have to break away from us in order to be the individuals God plans for them to be, Jesus had to break away from His sonship under Mary. Remember when, from the cross, He said to her and His disciple John, *"Dear woman, here is your son"* (John 19:26), meaning that John was to provide a home for her? Perhaps there is a deeper meaning. Anne Ortlund, in her book *My Sacrifice, His Fire*, suggests that in saying this, Christ was "actually making the final break in the physical relationship between [his mother and Him]." Anne explains further by quoting author Russell Bradley Jones: "[Mary] found that the salvation relationship is higher than the family relationship. She learned that it was better to have [Christ] as her Savior and Lord than to have Him as her son." He saved the best for last!

I have actually heard women after the first six weeks taking their baby to day care and saying, "Well, the baby doesn't do anything, really. I'm not missing anything." Wait just a minute! Now that you've reached the end of this grueling baby boot camp, you are soon to experience your baby's first smile. No one wants to miss that. Then the giggles. And soon he'll find his toes. (That's built-in entertainment for everyone.) Now that the adjustment to this earth-life has been completed, and your alien baby realizes he is a human (and you're beginning to agree), the fun starts! It begins with that first smile, right about now.

Graduation. A time for new beginnings. This is the end of your tenure at Baby Boot Camp, but it is the beginning of the rest of your life. The firsts have begun. It is time to get to know your baby, as he spends less time eating, crying, and dirtying diapers and more time exploring, observing, and imitating. It's time for peek-a-boo and rocky-horse. The end of the first six weeks. Breathe a sigh of relief: Whew! Praise God! You're a graduate.

❤

Thank God for new life with Jesus now and for His promised graduation to eternal life in Heaven still to come.